D1596785

A Spirituality of Ageing

A Spirituality of Ageing

MARK G. BOYER

WIPF & STOCK · Eugene, Oregon

A SPIRITUALITY OF AGEING

Wipf & Stock
An Imprint of Wipf and Stock Publishers
199 W. 8th Ave., Suite 3
Eugene, OR 97401

www.wipfandstock.com

ISBN 13: 978-1-62564-834-1

Manufactured in the U.S.A.   06/02/2014

Dedicated to
Peter & Clara Cartwright,
Rita Goodhead,
Jeanette Gushwa,
Sandi Hahn,
Marcia Jones,
Robert Marts,
Regina McIlrath,
and
Jerome & Margaret Pelzl,
all ageing friends from Shell Knob

... [T]here is great gain in godliness
combined with contentment;
for we brought nothing into the world,
so that we can take nothing out of it . . . .

—1 TIM 6:6-7

Contents

Abbreviations

Analects	*The Analects of Confucius*
2 Cor	Second Letter of Paul to the Corinthians, Christian Bible (New Testament)
Deut	Deuteronomy, Hebrew Bible (Old Testament)
Dhammapada	*The Dhammapada*
Doctrine and Covenants	*The Book of Doctrine and Covenants*
Eccl	Ecclesiastes, Hebrew Bible (Old Testament)
Exod	Exodus, Hebrew Bible, (Old Testament)
Gen	Genesis, Hebrew Bible (Old Testament)
Gos Thom	The Gospel of Thomas, *The Complete Gospels*
Inf Gos Jas	The Infancy Gospel of James, *The Complete Gospels*
John	The Gospel According to John, Christian Bible (New Testament)
Luke	The Gospel According to Luke, Christian Bible (New Testament)
2 Macc	Second Book of Maccabees, Old Testament (Apocrypha)
Prov	Proverbs, Hebrew Bible, (Old Testament)
Ps	Psalm, Book of Psalms, Hebrew Bible, (Old Testament)
Quran	*The Quran*
Rig Veda	*The Rig Veda*

Abbreviations

Rom	Letter of Paul to the Romans, Christian Bible (New Testament)
1 Sam	First Book of Samuel, Hebrew Bible, (Old Testament)
Sir	The Wisdom of Jesus Son of Sirach (Ecclesiasticus), Old Testament (Apocrypha)
1 Tim	First Letter of Timothy, Christian Bible (New Testament)
Tob	Book of Tobit, Old Testament (Apocrypha)
Treatise on Resurrection	The Treatise on the Resurrection, *The Nag Hammadi Library*
Wis	The Wisdom of Solomon, Old Testament (Apocrypha)

Bible Note

The Hebrew Bible consists of thirty-nine books accepted by Jews and Protestants as Holy Scripture. The Old Testament also contains those thirty-nine books plus seven to fifteen more books or parts of books called the Apocrypha or the Deuterocanonical Books; the Old Testament is accepted by Catholics and several other Christian denominations as Holy Scripture. The Christian Bible, consisting of 27 books, is also called the New Testament; it is accepted by Christians as Holy Scripture. Thus, in this work:

- Hebrew Bible (Old Testament) indicates that a book is found both in the Hebrew Bible and the Old Testament;

- Old Testament (Apocrypha) indicates that a book is found only in the Old Testament Apocrypha and not in the Hebrew Bible;

- and Christian Bible (New Testament) indicates that a book is found only in the Christian Bible or New Testament.

Introduction

AT SOME TIME AROUND the age of fifty—as early as forty or as late as sixty—most people come to terms with their age. They recognize that they have lived at least one half or more of their lives, and that the second half may be shorter than the first half! Most people refer to this process as ageing; the effects or the characteristics of getting older are more prominent. In upper level discourse this is often referred to as reaching maturity, although in some cases such language may indicate a denial of ageing.

Coming to terms with one's age is a process. At first a person denies it; that's why it may take a long time to accept one's accumulated number of years. "Sixty is the new forty," people often say. When asked how old one is, a standard "thirty-nine years old" is always given.

Because there are so many anti-ageing creams, laser procedures, and cosmetic surgeries available, looking younger can aid in denial. Everyone has heard an elderly person say, "You are only as old as you feel, and I feel like I'm forty!"

No matter how well one attempts to erase the signs of one's years, the effects of ageing often bring a person face-to-face with the length of his or her years and introduce the stage of rage and anger. "Ageing is not supposed to happen to me," an individual says to himself or herself. "Why am I experiencing diminishment?" People no longer hear the softer sounds they once heard without the aid of a hearing device. Foods and drinks do not taste the way they used to because the taste buds on the tongue have decreased. Likewise, odors that used to tickle the nose are no longer noticed. And touching contains much less sensation than used to be on the finger tips; it becomes easier to get burned or frost-bitten without

dulling of senses

even knowing it. Conversation becomes labored as the brain is searched for the right word that the person cannot think of at a certain moment. Glasses may be needed to see things and to read, whereas they were never needed before. Who wouldn't be angry at experiencing oneself falling apart?

The third stage of ageing is bargaining. After being urged by a spouse or friend to get a hearing aid, one will finally purchase it as long as it cannot be seen by others. One will never admit that his or her favorite food no longer tastes as good as it used to taste; therefore, there must be something wrong with the way it was prepared. Things get dropped and broken, but there is a reason: "My hands were wet. The statue fell off the table." A person can be heard to say, "I'll get contacts, but I'm not wearing glasses." That's bargaining.

As the human body continues to diminish with ageing, depression often sets in, especially after attempting a diet and failing, or beginning an exercise program and stopping, or getting a hearing aid and not wearing it. Muscles do not work the way they used to function. Skin becomes loose and wrinkly. Inner organs get diseased, arteries clog, joints ache. The ageing person spends more time with the doctor, may take many prescription drugs, and have to adhere to strict diets. Somewhere in this process, the ageing individual sooner or later comes face-to-face with death, the termination of life. And this adds even more depression.

Finally, one reaches acceptance. A person accepts the fact that he or she is fifty, fifty-five, sixty, sixty-five, or seventy years old and that most of life has already been lived. A peaceful resignation settles in that sets the individual free to live the rest of his or her years. One learns how to age gracefully. In other words, there is a spirituality of ageing, and, while it will be similar to others' spirituality, it will be uniquely each person's own.

The elderly embrace letting go to something that is bigger than they are. They come to realize that they are not the center of things, and they begin to submit to the diminishment that, ultimately, leads to death in the future. Some people go quietly through this process, while others battle it through every step. When the transformation is complete, a new phase of life is entered. It may

be characterized by a slower pace, lingering contemplation, acceptance of limitations, and a peace that leads to a deeper spirituality
that trusts that even in diminishment to death there is a freedom
of spirit that both surrounds and emanates from the person. In
other words, a person is awakened to his or her true identity; he or
she comes to realize that he or she has a divine nature.

In this book the reader will be led on a quest to explore a
personal spirituality of ageing. The equipment needed has been
gathered and is presented here. The words of wisdom from the
literature of the world's religions are sown throughout the pages of
this book. The reader is invited to linger wherever he or she finds
an interest.

This book is designed to be a type of workbook for the ageing. Each chapter is to be processed thoroughly before moving
on to the next chapter. Some readers may spend a day on each
exercise and finish the book in about a month. Other readers may
spend several days on an exercise in order to step carefully into the
depths of ageing presented by the exercise.

A universal process of ageing is presumed by the author. Because it is universal, various parts of the sacred literature of the
world's religions have been employed to illustrate the universal-
ity of the process. Thus, there is an ecumenical dimension to the
book. However, no matter how universal the ageing process may
be, each person develops his or her personal spirituality of ageing. By working through each exercise in this book, the reader will
arrive at a spirituality of ageing that he or she may not have been
aware of previously.

Four-part Exercise

This book consists of exercises in a fifteen-minute spirituality of
ageing. Any process takes time; the process of ageing is a graceful
sweep from one stage of life to another. Each of the first five chap-
ters in this book offers reflections organized into four parts which
will provide the reader with about a fifteen-minute reflection on
an aspect of a spirituality of ageing.

Introduction

The first part of each exercise is a short quotation from scripture from one of the world's religions. It focuses on one aspect of the topic of the chapter. The reflection, part two, explores the metaphor or idea found in the scripture passage for its meanings and makes some applications for today. In the journal section, part three, the reader makes connections between the sacred literature, the reflection, and his or her own life. Those connections may be written down or meditated on with the help of the questions. In order to prepare for chapter 6, which leads the reader in a process of gathering his or her deepest insights into his or her spirituality of ageing, the writer recommends that the reader record his or her thoughts in a journal (written or electronic). Once the reader is finished, the exercise is concluded with a short prayer.

The four-part process is called a spirituality of ageing, a way of preparing the self to grow in age, wisdom, and grace. Spirituality, as a way of life, transforms, transfigures, the person step-by-step as he or she gets closer and closer to the divine—however one chooses to name it. After meeting the divine, the individual better understands all of the circumstances of his or her life, including his or her unique self. Spirituality is the way that one is in the divine's presence, which emerges through human experiences of ageing and guided reflections upon those experiences.

Never can one imagine that he or she can be fully who he or she was created to be. However, through the ageing process of denial, anger, bargaining, depression, and acceptance, a person comes closer to human fulfillment and may erupt in joy at having reached many years of life.

chapter one

Denial

❦

If you have any doubt, O men [and women],
about being raised to life again,
(remember) that We created you from dust,
then a drop of semen, then an embryo, then a chewed up lump
of flesh shaped and shapeless,
that We may reveal (the various steps) to you.
We keep what We please in the womb for a certain time,
then you come out as a child,
then reach the prime of age.
Some of you die, some reach
the age of dotage where they forget
what they knew, having known it once.

—QURAN 22:5

Old Age at Hand

Scripture: "The Duke of She asked Tzu-lu about Master Kung (Confucius). Tsu-lu did not reply. The Master said, Why did you not say 'This is the character of the man: so intent upon enlightening the eager that he forgets his hunger, and so happy in doing so, that he forgets the bitterness of his lot and does not realize that old age is at hand. That is what he is'" (Analects VII:18).

Reflection: A Chinese adventurer, who gave himself the title of Duke of She, asks Tzu-lu about Confucius. When Tzu-lu does not answer the adventurer, Confucius presumes to reveal his own character to the Duke of She. He declares that he is so focused on teaching the ignorant, who want to learn, that he forgets that he is hungry. He is so delighted when he is able to enlighten others that he forgets the bitterness of his state in life; he doesn't even recognize that he is getting older.

When a person—even a teacher—fails to recognize that his or her older years are at hand, denial may be the cause. One can find all types of ways to deny age. "I don't feel like I am sixty-five years old," one person says. The presupposition in the statement is that there is a specific emotion that categorizes the elder years. "Sixty is the new forty," states another. The presupposition is that people are getting younger as they get older! "I can still do the work of a forty-year-old," states the eighty-year-old. And the presupposition is that there is a set amount of labor with which the eighty-year-old can match the forty-year-old. Laser surgery, cosmetic surgery, body hair removal, knee-, hip-, and rotator cuff-replacements, and other such techniques assist in the age-denial or old-age-forgetting process.

√ Some people forget about how old they are by continuing to work past retirement age. Some may need the money they make, but others use continued employment to deny their age. Others retire from their careers only to fill up their days with volunteer opportunities in an effort not to realize that old age is at hand.

In some cases, old age slaps one across the face with its glove, like a knight of old challenging another to a duel. A sudden fall on the ice with or without broken bones brings one face-to-face with age. A heart attack while shoveling snow off the driveway or sidewalk awakens a person to the fact that he or she is sixty-five, seventy, or seventy-five. A very active person is suddenly paralyzed by a stroke, and he or she must admit to his or her years.

The denial of one's age may not be overt. One may never say, "I'm not getting old." Denial may be covert. Like Confucius, a person does not realize that old age is at hand. The first step in developing a spirituality of ageing is to admit to the number of one's years.

JOURNAL/MEDITATION: In what specific ways do you deny your age?

PRAYER: My days pass quickly and come to an end, like a sigh, Great Teacher. Assist me in realizing the number of my years, that I may not be so focused on others that I fail to appreciate the shortness of my life. Amen.

Old Age Characteristics

SCRIPTURE: "Remember your creator in the days of your youth, before the days of trouble come, and the years draw near when you will say, 'I have no pleasure in them'; before the sun and the light and the moon and the stars are darkened and the clouds return with the rain; in the day when . . . the strong men are bent, and the women who grind cease working because they are few; . . . when one is afraid of heights . . . ; because all must go to their eternal home, and the mourners will go about the streets; . . . and the dust returns to the earth as it was, and the breath returns to God who gave it" (Eccl 12:1–3, 5, 7).

REFLECTION: The Hebrew Bible (Old Testament) Book of Ecclesiastes is classified as wisdom literature because it offers deep knowledge to those who read it. The author, who refers to himself as "the Teacher" (or "Qoheleth" or "the Preacher"), offers the advice that a person enjoy life and its pleasures as much as possible, as long as such enjoyment is informed by the inevitability of old age and death. The edited verses above come at the end of the book and emphasize the importance of facing one's age in order to prepare for death.

The Teacher exhorts his readers to remember their creator while they are young. In the Hebrew Bible (Old Testament), the creator is, of course, God, who breathes the breath of life into people. Using a variety of metaphors for old age, the author refers to the elder years as days of trouble in which people take no pleasure. Eyesight begins to fail. Tears stream down one's cheeks at the realization that he or she cannot see as well as he or she used to be able to see, that he or she cannot see in the dark.

In the older years, the men are stooped, the women can no longer work the long hours they used to toil, and both men and women are afraid of heights. Their days of climbing a ladder are long past; the days of stepping onto a stool to get things off of the highest shelf of the highest cabinet are over. The fear of a fall and broken bones takes precedence in one's life.

As the Preacher reflects on the end of human life, he states the obvious that all must go to their eternal home, that is, all must die. There will be mourners at each person's passing. But the inevitability of human life is that every person of dust—and that includes all people—returns to the earth. Another way to state this fact is to declare that one's life breath returns to God who gave it.

A spirituality of ageing includes facing days of trouble when nothing seems to go the way it should; fixing failing eyesight with glasses, lasers, or surgery; not being able to work as long as one used to; becoming stooped or shrinking in size; not climbing ladders or stools; and accepting the fact that one day a person will take his or her last breath and return to dust through burial or cremation. These things cannot be denied.

JOURNAL/MEDITATION: Which of the following do you deny: days of trouble, poor eyesight, shorter working hours, being stooped, climbing ladders or standing on stools, accepting death? What keeps you in denial?

PRAYER: Creator God, you breathe the breath of life into me at the moment of my conception in my mother's womb, and you fill me with your Spirit throughout my life. As I journey back to the dust out of which you formed me, remove all that hinders me from entering the eternal home you have prepared for me. Blessed is your name, now and forever. Amen.

Old Age Light Passage

SCRIPTURE: "This is the thunderbolt which often whirleth down from the lofty misty realm . . . . Beyond this realm there is another glory: so through old age they pass and feel no sorrow" (Rig Veda 10:27.21).

REFLECTION: From the sacred literature of Hinduism comes *The Rig Veda*, which means "praise knowledge" or "praise wisdom," a collection of over 1,000 hymns, each with numbered verses, divided into ten books. All totaled, there are over 10,000 verses in this oldest collection of sacred hymns intended to lead the reader into rational contemplation.

The verse above begins with the image of a lightning bolt, which flashes from the lofty misty realm of the sky when a massive electrostatic discharge between the electrically charged regions within clouds—or between one cloud and another cloud or between a cloud and the ground—occurs. A thunderbolt usually occurs when warm air is mixed with a cold air mass which results in an atmospheric disturbance that polarizes the atmosphere. The lightning flash indicates that the charged regions are once again temporarily equalized.

The wisdom taught by *The Rig Veda* is that beyond the sky is another realm. In ancient cosmology, the world was understood to be a three-storied universe. On the bottom story is where the dead lived. People lived on the second story. And the gods lived on the third story, located above the sky or the dome of the earth. Lightning gives those who live on the second story a peek into the top story. Just as lightning streaks from the top story to the middle story, so will those who pass through old age streak from the second story to the glory of the top story.

Another image imbedded in the verse employs the experience of mist or fog. A mist or fog often disappears as quickly as it appears. Such is life; it appears like a mist, and then it disappears like a mist. People pass through old age and should feel no sorrow, because they know that there is something for them in the other realm that a thunderbolt has revealed to them. Just like a lightning bolt flashes across the sky, so does the lifetime of every human being flash across the earth. A spirituality of ageing recognizes the shortness of life and hopes for a safe passage through old age to whatever is in the realm beyond it.

Journal/Meditation: In what ways do you deny the shortness of your life?

Prayer: Like lightning I have entered the world, and like lightning I will leave it. Grant me the wisdom, God of Light, to pass through these years without sorrow and so come to your light eternal. Amen.

Old Age Sleep Passage

Scripture: ". . . [I]t is appointed to [the faithful] to die at the age of man; wherefore children shall grow up until they become old, old men [and women] shall die; but they shall not sleep in the dust, but they shall be changed in the twinkling of an eye . . ." (*Doctrine and Covenants* 63:13).

REFLECTION: The *Book of Doctrine and Covenants* of the Reorganized Church of Jesus Christ of Latter Day Saints, commonly known as the Mormons, states that even the faithful who are declared righteous will age and die before they are changed at the Lord's coming. Those who store treasure in heaven by good works receive blessings now and rewards to come when old things pass away and all is made new by the Lord's coming.

The *Book of Doctrine and Covenants* presumes that there is a rhythm to life. Children are conceived by their parents, they are born, and they grow to adulthood; then, they become old and die at the age when people die. Of course, that age continues to change, due primarily to advances in modern medicine. Cholesterol drugs keep arteries from becoming blocked with plaque, and this in turn keeps heart attacks from happening. Quadruple heart bypass surgery is performed on eighty-four-year-olds to get blood to their hearts. Whereas cancer used to take the lives of its victims, drug therapy, radiation therapy, and chemotherapy add years to a person's life. Because of modern medicine, old age at thirty or forty in the first century has been extended to eighty or ninety in the twenty-first century.

Even though old men and women die, those who are righteous will not sleep in the dust of the earth. Because of the resurrection of Jesus Christ, those who die in him will be raised at his coming never to die again and receive their inheritance for having remained faithful throughout their lives, even into old age.

The *Book of Doctrine and Covenants* compares the passage through old age to one's daily routine of sleeping and waking. For seven, eight, or nine hours, most people go to bed and sleep, after which they awaken. Sleep is a naturally recurring state of altered consciousness, little sensory activity, and inactivity of most muscles. Sleep enables the body to repair itself, fight disease, and conserve energy. Just as people pass through sleep to wakefulness, so those righteous who pass through the old age of sleep will be changed in a twinkling of an eye when the Lord comes to awaken them to new life.

A spirituality of ageing must include some reflection on old age that leads to death and beyond. Just like sleep is universal in the human kingdom, so is old age and death. Old age leads to death. However, those who believe in the resurrection of Jesus Christ hope for life beyond death. Their hope is grounded in the daily experience of sleep—old age leading to death—and awakening—leading to regenerated life.

Journal/Meditation: What is the current length of years of men and women in your family? How can advanced years foster denial of ageing?

Prayer: Lord Jesus, you overcame the world through your resurrection. As one of your followers, grant that I may age in grace in your sight and be found worthy of life when you come in glory to raise the righteous, who will live with you forever and ever. Amen.

Old Age Attributes

Scripture: "If you gathered nothing in your youth, how can you find anything in your old age? How attractive is sound judgment in the gray-haired, and for the aged to possess good counsel! How attractive is wisdom in the aged, and understanding and counsel in the venerable! Rich experience is the crown of the aged, and their boast is the fear of the Lord" (Sir 25:3–6).

Reflection: Sirach, otherwise known as Ecclesiasticus or the Wisdom of Jesus Son of Sirach in the Old Testament (Apocrypha), is a collection of Hebrew wisdom teachings coming from a scribe around 180 BCE. In the above passage, the author teaches that one's youth is the time for gathering wisdom. If a person has become truly wise in his or her youth, then he or she will have wisdom in old age. In other words, to become wise one must begin early.

Sirach presents five attributes of wisdom in old age. The first is sound judgment, an opinion with authority that comes only with old age and the practice of discernment. The second is good counsel, advice that is given after careful consultation and deliberation practiced over many years. Understanding is the third attribute; one who understands grasps the meaning of something and is able to express his or her reasonableness with the certainty that comes only with age. The fourth attribute is rich experience, that is, direct observation of life's events and/or participation in them with deep reflection upon them. And the fifth attribute of wisdom is the fear of the Lord, a state of profound reverence and awe toward God which grows from one's youth to one's older years as a person comes to a broader perspective of his or her place in the universe.

According to Sirach, those attributes of wisdom should be sought in one's younger years so that a person can be wise in his or her older years. In a culture that celebrates youth and despises age, Sirach's words can serve as an antidote. Childhood and youth are being stretched into the late twenties and early thirties. Adult children are often just that—children. They have not yet grown up and taken their place in the world. Many continue to live with their parents. When Sirach was writing about wisdom, childhood and youth ended around the age of thirteen, when most people married and began to raise a family. Thus, for Sirach the gathering of wisdom takes place within the first decade of one's life; today, it takes place in the first three decades of one's life, if it takes place at all.

While people today live longer and have many more years of childhood and youth than people of two millennia ago, there is no evidence that they have gathered sound judgment, good counsel, understanding, rich experience, or fear of the Lord. Sirach knows that these attributes of old age have to be gathered intentionally in youth. Otherwise, one reaches old age without the benefits of wisdom. This can lead to the denial of one's years, because a person continues to function as if he or she is twenty-five when in fact he or she is sixty-five or seventy-five.

Journal/Meditation: For each of the following attributes indicate how you gathered it in your youth: sound judgment, good counsel, understanding, rich experience, fear of the Lord.

Prayer: Blessed are you, Lord, God of all creation. You fill men and women with wisdom. Teach me sound judgment; give me good counsel; and help me to understand your ways through reflection upon the rich experiences of my life. Grant that I may reverence and fear your name, forever and ever. Amen.

chapter two

Anger

It is God who created you of weakness,
then after weakness gave you strength,
then after strength will give you weakness and gray hair.
Surely He makes whatever He wills.
He is all-knowing and all-powerful.

—QURAN 30:54

Premature Old Age

SCRIPTURE: "Do not give yourself over to sorrow, and do not distress yourself deliberately. A joyful heart is life itself, and rejoicing lengthens one's life span. Indulge yourself and take comfort, and remove sorrow far from you, for sorrow has destroyed many, and no advantage ever comes from it. Jealousy and anger shorten life, and anxiety brings on premature old age" (Sir 30:21–24).

REFLECTION: The Old Testament's (Apocrypha's) 180 BCE reflection on wisdom of Jesus son of Sirach, otherwise called Ecclesiasticus, advises against sorrow in one's older years. In fact, deep distress and regret lead to premature old age. Sadness, a type of sorrow, can be seen on the face of one diagnosed with cancer. Grief, another type of sorrow, seems to be etched into the being of a surviving spouse after many, many years of marriage. Anguish, still another type of sorrow, sets in with the dread of losing a job, a home, or a car. Inconsolable misery, another kind of sorrow, is the woe of parents who lose children to gunfire in schools; this sorrow can destroy them. And regret, caused by deep disappointment with oneself or others, leaves a person in a state of sorrow. To understand these aspects of sorrow all one needs to do is watch the evening news on television or read the daily newspaper.

Sorrow of any kind results in anger. Sirach advocates hope instead of depressive sorrow. The antidote to sorrow is a joyful heart, which can add years to one's life. And a joyful heart can be had by enjoying the good things in life. It all depends on one's attitude or perspective. Instead of sadness, a cancer patient can be happy to take advantage of medical knowledge that did not exist five or ten years ago. Instead of grief, a mourning spouse can take time to establish relationships with others who have lost a spouse in death. The loss of a job, a home, or a car does not have to result in anguish; it can be the occasion for simple living. Many parents have turned their inconsolable misery, caused by the death of their children, into efforts at gun control. Instead of regret, a person can turn his or her disappointment into an opportunity to learn from his or her mistakes.

Besides sorrow, Sirach also writes about jealousy, anger, and anxiety. Jealousy describes one who is intolerant of rivalry. One person has something that another does not have; one person has a relationship with another person that a third person does not enjoy. A jealous disposition consumes an individual's life.

Likewise, anger shortens one's life. Anger is a feeling of displeasure with oneself or with others, and it usually evolves into antagonism, in which case one's spiritual energy is spent on being upset about something or with someone.

Anxiety, a painful or apprehensive uneasiness of mind over an impending or anticipated ill, not only shortens life, but brings on premature old age. Some people spend most of their time worrying about what could happen instead of what is happening.

Sirach's words of wisdom about a balanced life, focused on a joyful and grateful heart, does not stop the ageing process. However, it does supply a spirituality of ageing that helps a person's spirit rise above all that which seems to rob one of life: sorrow, distress, jealousy, anger, and anxiety.

JOURNAL/MEDITATION: In what specific ways do sorrow, distress, jealousy, anger, and anxiety rob you of life?

PRAYER: Lord God, you give those who trust in you a joyful heart and length of years. Remove sorrow, distress, jealousy, anger, and anxiety from my life, and grant me the grace of rejoicing in you all my days. You live and reign forever and ever. Amen.

The Path

SCRIPTURE: "Even now [the one who finds the path that leads directly forward] breathed: these days hath he remembered. . . . Yet in his youth old age hath come upon him: he hath grown gracious, good, and free from anger" (Rig Veda 10:32.8).

REFLECTION: According to Hinduism's *The Rig Veda*, once a person finds the path he or she needs to walk through life, he or she begins to show signs of life, namely, breathing. This book of sacred wisdom betrays a depth of knowledge that many may never attain. Indeed, until a person finds his or her path in the world, he or she has not yet become fully alive.

Those who have found a path, a career, a job, a spouse, a family, a home, etc. are content and happy in being who they are and in what they do. Their lives are full of what really matters. In the words of *The Rig Veda*, even now they breathe the air of the depth of life. They are wise ahead of their years. They can be contrasted to those who have not yet found a path through life.

The lost and indecisive often wonder who they are; every few years they change careers or jobs. They cannot find a suitable spouse or settle down by buying a home and raising a family. Whatever will make them happy is often further into the future. They have not yet begun to breathe, and if they do not get to the point where they do, they will become the walking dead.

Those who have found a path and breathe have also achieved a wisdom of old age in their youth. The wisdom that usually characterizes those who are older has taken root and is growing in the lives of youth who travel their paths forward. They possess a definition of themselves which is always in the process of development. Reliability, stability, and capability characterize their lives. They pass through life graciously, good, and free from anger, in the words of *The Rig Veda*.

Furthermore, those who have found their path keep growing graciously into their older years, that is, they are marked by kindness and courtesy. They grow goodly, that is, they are pleasantly attractive. And they are free from anger, that is, they possess no displeasure or antagonism.

A spirituality of ageing must include a path, a direction, a purpose that both informs an individual and prods him or her forward. In the older years, the person remembers the path he or she has walked, even as he or she continues to grow gracious, good, and free from anger.

JOURNAL/MEDITATION: Specifically, how have you grown gracious, good, and free from anger?

PRAYER: Grant that I may grow gracious, good, and free from anger as I walk the path that brings joy to my life. May I always breathe deeply of past memories, even as I bring to life new ones. Grant that my journey may praise the wisdom of the ages. Amen.

Wasting Away

SCRIPTURE: "Quiet wasted away in this form, A nest for disease, perishable. This putrid accumulation breaks up. For life has its end in death" (Dhammapada XI:148).

REFLECTION: Chapter XI of *The Dhammapada*, Buddhism's sacred writing, is a reflection on old age. This book of the path to virtue presents religiously inspiring statements thought to have been made by the Buddha on various occasions. While Buddha taught orally in the sixth century BCE, *The Dhammapada* was not written until several centuries later.

The body quietly wastes away in its current form due to old age. Like a bird's nest in which eggs are laid and new life is hatched, in old age the body becomes a nest for diseases that renders it perishable. In fact, from the moment of birth, the body begins to perish; this is clearly seen in old age. The putrid accumulation is always in the process of breaking up or rotting; this can be deduced from observing the matter that emerges from the body's nine orifices (ears, eyes, nostrils, mouth, anus, urethral opening). The complete breakup of the body's life will come to an end in death. Indeed, the life of all beings has its end in death.

One's older years bring a person closer and closer to the end of life. An individual can relish these older years and the process in which they end, or one can be angry that they lead to death. Some people choose to age quietly, while others express anger at their accumulation of knowledge and learning breaking up through Alzheimer's Disease. Anger erupts at the accumulation of muscle breaking up and hanging on a bony frame, at the accumulation of rogue cells breaking up healthy tissues with some form of cancer, at the accumulation of stomach acid that not only breaks up food but gives one heartburn. Anger prepares for a battle with the inevitable, which, as *The Dhammapada*, states, is death.

A spirituality of ageing must take into account the wasting away of the perishable bodily form. Denial is the usual first response. Denial is followed by anger. As the older years are uncovered, the accumulation breaks up, and life ends in death.

JOURNAL/MEDITATION: With what aspect of your bodily deterioration are you most angry?

PRAYER: As I quietly waste away in age through disease, I look forward to a new form. May my anger at my gradual dying be spent as I look forward to joining my ancestors in death. Amen.

Bodily Decay

SCRIPTURE: "Even well-decked royal chariots wear away; And the body too falls into decay. But the dhamma of the good ones goes not to decay, For the good speak [of it] with the good" (Dhammapada XI:151).

REFLECTION: Buddhism's sacred writing, *The Dhammapada*, contains a chapter of eleven poetic strophes on old age. *Dhamma* means "virtue," in terms of right living, and *pada* means "path." Thus, this book of the path to virtue presents religiously inspiring statements thought to have been made by the Buddha, Siddhartha Gautama, on various occasions. While the Buddha taught orally in the sixth century BCE, *The Dhammapada* was not written until several centuries later.

The Buddha, meaning "the awakened one" or "the enlightened one," begins with the observation that even the precious-jeweled, royal chariots wear out—as do all other things—so, too, the human body decays. What does not decay is virtue that transcends the world. Those who have reached this state of existence, such as the Buddha, are able to speak of it with others who have similarly become wise.

The path to *dhamma* or transcendent virtue is awareness or awakening to the desires that cause suffering. Awareness eliminates desire, and when desire is eliminated, so is suffering. When a person reaches the sublime state of total awareness or virtue, he or she has achieved nirvana, peace.

Suffering, anxiety, or unease can be physical or mental. As one ages, a person attempts to hold on to things that are constantly changing by craving or desiring them, and this causes suffering. Recognizing that all forms of life are impermanent, a person is set free from desire and the ignorance that stuff gives value to one's life. What is of real value is that which endures even through bodily decay—and that is virtue.

Walking the path of enlightened virtue involves right understanding, right intention, right speech, right action, right livelihood, right effort, right mindfulness, and right concentration. These are not stages, but interconnected dimensions of a person's being that define a way of living virtuously.

All things, no matter how noble, beautiful, or royal they are, decay. A spirituality of ageing acknowledges this fact, but it also declares that one's way of life, a person's virtue, does not decay. Those who have achieved nirvana speak of virtue with others who have also achieved it. Anger at bodily decay may cause some of the suffering of old age, but virtue can transcend it.

JOURNAL/MEDITATION: What anger do you have in your older years? How can accepting your bodily decay help you eliminate some suffering from your life?

PRAYER: Aware that all suffering is desire, I pray that through meditation I may reach a state of pure virtue. Then, my way of life will demonstrate to others that bodily decay in old age is not to be feared, but to be embraced. Amen.

Led by Others

Scripture: "Jesus said to Peter, 'Very truly, I tell you, when you were younger, you used to fasten your own belt and to go wherever you wished. But when you grow old, you will stretch out your hands, and someone else will fasten a belt around you and take you where you do not wish to go'" (John 21:18).

Reflection: John's Gospel in the Christian Bible (New Testament) has two endings. To the original ending was added an additional chapter which contains an account of a miraculous catch of fish by the disciples—which is similar to a story appearing at the call of the disciples in Luke's Gospel (5:1–11)—and a rehabilitation-of-Peter account in which the apostle three times affirms his love for the resurrected Christ in order to undo his three-fold denial of Jesus earlier in the story. The above proverbial passage is found at the end of Peter's triple profession of love.

A proverb is a brief, popular epigram or maxim which summarizes a truth. There are economic, medical, political, religious, etc. proverbs. Over time, these short sayings become so summarized that their original meanings and applications are forgotten, or, because of their place in literature, they become limited. Such is the case for the above-mentioned proverb; in its context it is understood by the author of John's Gospel to refer to Peter's death. However, if it is unpacked, it can shed light on understanding the anger that often accompanies old age.

The proverb is divided into two parts. The first part deals with youth. When a person is young, he or she dresses himself or herself and goes wherever he or she desires. The culture-bound proverb refers to this as fastening one's belt. However, when a person grows old, he or she may no longer be able to dress himself or herself and needs assistance. The culture-bound proverb refers to this as stretching out one's hands and having someone else fasten a belt around one and take the person where he or she does not wish to go—which causes the older person to be angry.

When an elderly person is no longer able to operate a motor vehicle safely, adult children or someone else must take away his or her car keys in order both to protect the person and others who may be in danger when the elderly person gets behind the steering wheel. Unless one hands over the keys willingly, anger is the result. Now, the person is dependent upon others to get to the doctor, the grocery store, the hair salon, etc.

The proverb becomes even more applicable when a person's ability to walk is curtailed by old age. A wheel chair signals dependency. Now, not only is the person not able to drive to the places he or she used to go, but he or she is not able to get from one room to another on his or her feet. This, too, can cause anger to erupt.

Assisted living arrangements further enhance the fact that an older person is not able to take care of himself or herself. And assisted living may be followed by residence in a nursing home, often signaling complete dependence upon others to take one where he or she may not want to go, like the dining room, the television room, the community room, etc. After being strapped into a wheel chair, anger may be the result as one is brought to places he or she may not desire to go.

A spirituality of ageing must consider gradual dependency upon others. Remembering one's youth, when a person was able to dress himself or herself and go wherever he or she pleased, does not help a person to accept the limitations of one's older years. In the older years, a person may need to accept the fact that he or she cannot dress himself or herself, is often taken to where he or she would not like to go, and that anger is not the best response to such dependency upon others.

JOURNAL/MEDITATION: In what ways are you dependent upon others? What anger may lurk under your dependency?

PRAYER: From my dependency upon others, O God, teach me submission to you. Grant that the freedom of my youth may lead gracefully to the captivity of my older years. Remove all anger and bitterness from my life. Hear me in the name of Jesus Christ, my Lord. Amen.

chapter three

Bargaining

It is God who created you from dust,
then from a sperm,
then formed you into pairs.
Neither does a female conceive
nor gives birth without His knowledge;
nor do the old grow older or become younger in years
but in accordance with the law (of nature).
Indeed the law of God works inevitably.

—QURAN 35:11

Lengthened Life

SCRIPTURE: "I have declared your wondrous deeds, O Asvins: may this be mine, and many kine and heroes. May I, enjoying lengthened life, still seeing, enter old age as 'twere the house I live in" (Rig Veda 1:116.25).

REFLECTION: Hinduism's *The Rig Veda*, meaning "praise knowledge" or "praise wisdom," contains fifty-seven hymns dedicated to Asvins (or Ashvins), divine twin horsemen, representing the shining of sunrise and sunset. In Hindu mythology they are depicted with human bodies and horse heads, appearing in the sky before dawn in a golden chariot, bringing treasures to men and averting misfortune and sickness. They are like the Dioscuri (Castor and Pollux), twins of Greek and Roman mythology.

The singer of the hymn reminds the twins that because he has declared their wondrous deeds in the previous twenty-four strophes of his hymn, they should grant him what he asks, namely, to be declared master of the place where he is composing the hymn, to be given many cattle (kine), and to be given many heroes. In Hinduism a hero is a person who has been assimilated to a god by identifying him with an incarnation of that god; thus, great religious teachers are often considered manifestations of the god of their devotional preaching, possessing and using the powers of the god. The hymn-writer continues to bargain by asking for a long life with good eyesight and old age that becomes him, like the house in which he lives.

While this poet is Hindu, he reflects a theme woven through other sacred writings. Many religious observers bargain with the god, the gods, or the God they worship. A bargain is an agreement between parties settling what each gives or receives in a transaction between them. Thus, the hymn-writer praises the Asvins in exchange for riches, cows, heroes, a long life, and easy old age.

What is true of Hymn 116, verse 25, of Book 1 of *The Rig Veda* remains true today. People often bargain with a god, the gods, God, the LORD, Allah, Jesus, etc. Often, they promise to change the way they live their lives if their cancer is successfully removed by surgery or sent into remission by chemotherapy. They set aside nine days of prayer (a novena) to implore the deity for all kinds of favors. Imploring their god or God for help, they promise to help the poor, work in a soup kitchen, or become a minister in service to a god or God.

As people age, like the hymn-writer quoted from above, they bargain for a longer life with good eyesight. They want to age gracefully so that no one, including them, will even notice. They will enter old age as if they were entering their home, if they can get the better part of the bargain.

JOURNAL/MEDITATION: What bargain concerning ageing have you made with your god, gods, God, LORD, Allah, Jesus, etc.?

PRAYER: O Divinity, I have declared your wondrous deeds. Grant me riches, and give me heroes after whom to model my life. May I, enjoying lengthened life, still seeing, enter old age as if I were entering the house in which I live. Amen.

Honor Father and Mother

SCRIPTURE: ". . . [T]he Lord honors a father above his children, and he confirms a mother's right over her children. Those who respect their father will have long life, and those who honor their mother obey the Lord . . . . My child, help your father in his old age, and do not grieve him as long as he lives; even if his mind fails, be patient with him; because you have all your faculties do not despise him. Whoever forsakes a father is like a blasphemer, and whoever angers a mother is cursed by the Lord" (Sir 3:2, 6, 12–13, 16).

REFLECTION: In his reflection on the fourth commandment to honor one's father and one's mother, Jesus, son of Sirach, writing in the second century BCE, exhorts his reader to honor his or her father, especially in his older years. A patriarchal culture, such as that in which Sirach was written, honors only men and shames women. A man cannot be shamed, and a woman cannot be honored in a patriarchal culture. This is why a father is mentioned so often and honored *above* his children in the passage, while a mother's right is mentioned seldom and confirmed *over* her children.

The patriarchal culture which produced the Old Testament (Apocrypha) is not the culture lived in today. So, this reflection will include both father and mother. Parents need to be cared for in their old age. Children should not cause their parents to suffer by living scandalous lives, by addictive behavior, by not growing into adulthood, by abandoning them. Even if parents' minds fail because of age, Alzheimer's disease, or some other problem, children should be patient with them in conversation, in nursing home life, in hospitalization. Adult children, who possess all their faculties, should not despise their parents.

While adult children may perceive that they are honoring their parents by taking care of them and making decisions for them, parents may perceive that their adult children have taken control of their lives and bargain for the right to make their own decisions. Parents often bargain with their children not to have to go into a nursing home, promising anything to stay out of such an institution. Parents often bargain with their adult children not to go to the hospital where they may die. And, of course, parents bargain with their adult children not to take away their car keys, promising to get a driver or to drive only when absolutely necessary.

When the adult child becomes the parent (needing to make decisions for others) and the parent becomes the child (unable to make good decisions), some adult children forsake their parents because of the hurt feelings that result. The tectonic plates of relationships collide, and what should be a time to honor parents often becomes a time for fighting with them.

A spirituality of ageing needs to include room for honor of parents by adult children. In old age, parents often need help in making solid decisions concerning their future, and their adult children can honor them by helping them discern the best course of action to take. In old age, parents often need help cleaning their homes, and their adult children can honor them by mopping, vacuuming, and dusting. Permitting an adult child to transport parents to the doctor, the grocery store, or shopping mall also gives the adult child the opportunity to honor his or her parents.

In a patriarchal culture, God honors a father *above* his children, and, after a father, the Lord confirms a mother's right *over* her children. Children who respect their father will have long life, and those who honor their mother obey the Lord. Today, adult children still have the opportunity to honor their parents in their older years, and parents have the opportunity to let their adult children honor them.

JOURNAL/MEDITATION: How do/did you honor your parents in their older years? In what ways do/did they permit you to honor them in their old age? What bargains do/did they present to you?

PRAYER: Lord God, you honor parents above their children, and you promise long life to those children who honor their parents. Grant that I may be honored in my old age by my children as long as I live, even if my mind fails. Give my children patience and the ability to discern what is best for me. Here me through Jesus Christ, your Son, who honors you forever and ever. Amen.

Kind Old Age Days

SCRIPTURE: "Give us not up as prey to death, O Soma: still let us look upon the Sun arising. Let our old age with passing days be kindly. Let Nirrti depart to distant places" (Rig Veda 10:49.4).

REFLECTION: In Hymn 49 in chapter 10 of Hinduism's *The Rig Veda*, the poet asks for soma, a ritual drink prepared by extracting juice from the stalks of a no-longer-identifiable plant. He asks for this drink in order to keep those for whom he prays from becoming a prey to death, so that they can continue to watch the sun rise. He also asks that the passing days of their old age be kind to them. The refrain, which concludes most of the verses of this hymn, "Let

Nirrti depart to distant places," asks that the goddess of death and corruption depart to a faraway place.

In another hymn, 37, in book 10, the poet refers specifically to his writing as an invocation, a prayer, stating: "This invocation, these our words may Heaven and Earth, and Indra and the Waters and the Maruts hear. Ne'er may we suffer want in [the] presence of the Sun, and, living happy lives, may we attain old age" (Rig Veda 10:37.6). The invocation is addressed to Indra, the god of rain and thunderstorms and the supreme deity, and the Maruts (also Marutas), storm deities, along with heaven, earth, and water. Like 10:49.4 above, this prayer asks the various gods to set free the pray-er from need under the sun by supplying the rain necessary to make things grow and to live a happy life, even into old age.

The verses of both hymns are petitions or bargains with the gods. Both verses ask that death be far away and that one's days in old age be kind or happy. These ancient petitions from thousands of years ago are similar to the bargains people make today. "I don't mind getting old as long as I can put food on my table," an invocation declares. "I just want to have my health in my old age," another bargainer states. "As long as I can get along, I'll be happy in old age," states another petitioner.

Asking for old age to be free from want with happy days under the sun represents a step in the process of coming to terms with old age and developing a spirituality of ageing. At first the bargainer acknowledges that he or she is getting older, but then immediately qualifies it by seeking to live as if he or she is not getting older—by continuing to work to put food on the table, by being as healthy as one was in youth, and by getting along as a person did in years past. Today's bargaining is not all that different from that found in *The Rig Veda*, in which the petitioner seeks kindly days in old age with death far in the future and lack of want with a happy life into old age.

JOURNAL/MEDITATION: What bargains do you attempt to make to enjoy kind and happy days in old age with death far in the future?

PRAYER: May I not be a prey to death, but enjoy kind and happy days in my old age, free from want. Also, grant that I may bask in the warmth of the sun from its rising to its setting until I attain fullness of years. Amen.

Gift of a Day

SCRIPTURE: ". . . [A]ll our days pass away under your wrath [, Lord]; our years come to an end like a sigh. The days of our life are seventy years, or perhaps eighty, if we are strong; even then their span is only toil and trouble; they are soon gone, and we fly away. So teach us to count our days that we may gain a wise heart" (Ps 90:9–10, 12).

REFLECTION: While the Hebrew Bible's (Old Testament's) Psalm 90 is attributed to a prayer of Moses, the man of God, in its superscription, it is a hymn composed during the Babylonian Exile of the Jews which began in 587 BCE. The psalmist notes that days spent in captivity pass away under the Lord's wrath, a poetic way of referring to the experience of finitude. In other words, Jews are dying in exile; their days of life are ending with no hope of being set free to return to Jerusalem. Like the quickness of a person's sigh, so do the years of the captives came to an end.

The lyrics of the song mention the life-span of seventy or eighty years. When the poet was composing this song, few people lived to be seventy or eighty; the average life was thirty to forty years. That is why most people got married when they were twelve or thirteen and began to raise a family. If they were lucky, they might get to see their grandchildren. Few people ever lived to be seventy or eighty, even if they were strong; and even then they still had to work because there was no such thing as retirement. No matter how many years one reached, death caused everyone, ultimately, to disappear.

In the midst of these depressing lyrics about getting old, the psalmist bargains with the Lord, asking him to teach the exiles that every day is a gift, an opportunity to acquire a wise heart.

Hopefully, as an individual counts his or her days, he or she also counts wisdom, even in exile!

Indeed, coming to terms with one's older years and finitude can be a depressing reflection! And bargaining with God may be the occasion to gain hope. A spirituality of ageing often includes some type of bargaining. In exchange for one thing from God, the bargainer promises something to the Lord. In this poem, the bargainer, who can see no hope to the end of captivity—or finitude—asks God to teach the exiles to count their days as gifts given by a gracious Lord. If they do this, they can gain a wise heart, even in captivity.

The applications of the words of this psalm are many. Indeed, days pass quickly in one's older years. A person sighs, and another year has passed. Today, many people live to be seventy or eighty. However, because many retired people have had to return to the ranks of the employed for economic reasons, their days are full of toil and trouble, either part-time or full-time. One can ask the Lord to teach him or her to count his or her days that he or she may gain a wise heart.

A wise heart is one that knows what to do in almost every circumstance. The wise heart understands people, things, events, and situations and is able to take the right course of action. Wisdom implies the application of universal principles, values, reason, and knowledge. A person with a wise heart knows the ways of God and follows them. A wise heart disposes a person to apply right actions to truth in any circumstance. So, gaining wisdom of heart should be the object of the days in one's older years.

JOURNAL/MEDITATION: How have you dealt with your finitude? What bargaining was involved? In what specific ways do you have a wise heart?

PRAYER: As my days pass away, O Lord, and my years come to an end like a sigh, with your Spirit guide me through the toil and trouble of life. Grant me seventy or eighty years in your service, while you teach me to count my days and gain a wise heart. When

I am gone, grant me eternal life with you, who are one God, forever and ever. Amen.

Happy Fortune

SCRIPTURE: "I take thy hand in mine for happy fortune that thou mayst reach old age with me thy husband. Gods . . . have given thee to be my household's mistress" (Rig Veda 10:85.36).

REFLECTION: In Book 10 of *The Rig Veda*, a Hindu bridegroom addresses his Hindu bride in Hymn 85. Taking her hand in his, he declares hope for the happy fortune of them reaching old age together. The gods have given the bride to the groom to serve as mistress of his house.

Two points are worthy of reflection. The first is that the groom hopes for the happy fortune of reaching old age with his bride. The words echo the standard marriage vows in which each party promises to be true to each other in good times and bad times, in sickness and in health, and to love and honor each other all the days of their lives. Another version of marriage vows states that the couple takes each other to have and to hold, from the day of their marriage, for better, for worse, for richer, for poorer, in sickness and in health, until death parts them. The presupposition is that husband and wife will reach old age together.

The second point worthy of reflection concerns the will of the gods. The groom declares that the four gods (omitted from the above scripture passage)—Aryaman, Bhaga, Savitar, and Purandhi—have given the bride to the groom to manage his household. Aryaman, whose name means "bosom friend" or "companion," serves as a witness to Hindu marriage. Meaning "lord" or "patron," Bhaga is the god of wealth and marriage, while Savitar is the rouser or vivifier god. Finally, Purandhi is the goddess of childbirth. Thus, the gods of companionship, wealth, life, and childbirth are credited with the marriage in the same way as husband and wife promise to remain together through riches and poverty and sickness and health until death.

Very seldom do both parties of a marriage die at the same time. Although, there are cases in which diseases, natural disasters, and mutual suicides bring the lives of both people to an end at the same time. In old age, one person may bargain for the life of the other. One individual may ask to die first in order not to have to deal with the death of the other spouse. A person may pray that he or she does not live long enough to develop Alzheimer's disease or some crippling sickness. In other words, reaching a happy old age together is the desire of young people when they marry, but that desire is tempered by the life experiences that lead to and comprise old age.

JOURNAL/MEDITATION: If you are or were married, what bargaining have you done in your older years?

PRAYER: May I enjoy the happy fortune of reaching old age with the person I love. Grant that I may remain true to my spouse in good times and in bad times, in sickness and in health, and love and honor him or her all the days of my life. Amen.

chapter four

Depression

It is [the Lord] who created you from dust,
then a drop of semen, then the embryo;
afterwards He brings you forth as a child;
then you attain the age of manhood [or womanhood],
and then reach old age.
But some of you die before you reach the appointed term
that you may haply understand.
It is He who gives you life and death.
When He creates a thing, He has only to say:
"Be," and it is.

—QURAN 40:67-68

Wasting Away

Scripture: ". . . [W]e know that the one who raised the Lord Jesus will raise us also with Jesus, and will bring us with you [, Corinthians,] into his presence. Yes, everything is for your sake, so that grace, as it extends to more and more people, may increase thanksgiving, to the glory of God. So we do not lose heart. Even though our outer nature is wasting away, our inner nature is being renewed day by day. For this slight momentary affliction is preparing us for an eternal weight of glory beyond all measure . . ." (2 Cor 4:14–17).

Reflection: In his Second Letter to the Corinthians in the Christian Bible (New Testament), Paul addresses the depression that often accompanies the acceptance of getting older. At some point in their lives, people reach the stage where they acknowledge that they have counted fifty, sixty, seventy, or eighty years; they have lived most of their lives, and not many years remain. Such awareness is often accompanied by depression.

Paul addresses this depression with the assurance that God, who raised Jesus from the dead, will also raise the Corinthians—and those who read the letter written to the Corinthians—from the dead into God's presence. The apostle tells the Corinthians not to lose heart—not to be depressed—even though they experience their bodies wasting away or ageing. Grace, God's own life, is extended to more and more people to renew their inner nature. In a manner of speaking, as the body is deteriorating, the soul is growing. This natural, outer wasting away—or ageing—prepares people for supernatural, inner glory that cannot be measured, but has already been revealed in the resurrection of the Lord Jesus. Recognizing the growth of inner, spiritual grace leads to more and more thanksgiving to the glory of God.

Basically, the depression caused by ageing is sadness at the inevitable conclusion to life. Such sadness may be accompanied by inactivity, difficulty in thinking and concentration, an increase or decrease in appetite and time spent sleeping, feelings of dejection and hopelessness, and sometimes suicidal tendencies. The elderly may stop doing routine things and spend most of the day sitting in a chair. Some forget easily, failing to remember what they went to get from one room to the next. Eating so little as to lose weight or eating so much as to gain weight indicates depression. Likewise, when an elderly person sleeps less or more, he or she has entered into the stage of depression. Social isolation can bring on feelings of no one cares, and the result may be that there is no hope past sixty, seventy, or eighty years of age.

The outer nature is wasting away. The elderly are not as strong as they used to be. They cannot do the work they used to do. Lifting heavy objects may no longer be possible. Mowing the lawn may be too taxing. A longer response time may curtail driving a motor vehicle. These and many more indicators of bodily wasting away bring older people to a state of depression.

JOURNAL/MEDITATION: What are the indicators of depression for you?

PRAYER: Almighty God, you raised Jesus from the dead, and you promise to bring me into his presence. Fill me with your grace so that I do not lose heart, even though my outer nature is wasting away. Renew my inner nature through the Lord Jesus, your Son, who lives and reigns with you and the Holy Spirit, one God, forever and ever. Amen.

Unable to Separate

SCRIPTURE: "Who will separate us from the love of Christ? Will hardship, or distress, or persecution, or famine, or nakedness, or peril, or sword? No, in all these things we are more than conquerors through him who loved us. For I [, Paul,] am convinced that neither death, nor life, nor angels, nor rulers, nor things present, nor things to come, nor powers, nor height, nor depth, nor anything else in all creation, will be able to separate us from the love of God in Christ Jesus our Lord" (Rom 8:35, 37–39).

REFLECTION: In this passage from the Letter to the Romans in the Christian Bible (New Testament), Paul begins with the great deed that God did in Jesus, namely, raise him from the dead. The resurrection of the dead Jesus by God demonstrates God's love. Furthermore, resurrection shows that God did not abandon Jesus, his own Son. Therefore, God will not abandon those who are in Christ Jesus through faith.

Nothing can separate believers from the love of Christ, according to Paul. Hardship, anything causing suffering or privation, cannot separate people from Christ. Distress, any type of strain or difficulty, cannot separate people from Christ. The love of Christ cannot be severed by persecution, suffering because of belief; by famine, extreme scarcity of food; by nakedness, lack of clothing; by peril, exposure to the risk of being injured, destroyed, or lost; by the sword, a weapon with a long blade.

Paul is convinced that death cannot separate people from God's love, and neither can life. Angels and rulers of any kind cannot separate people from God's love. Even present events and future events do not have that ability. There is no height, nor depth, nor anything else in all creation that can separate people from the love of God in Christ Jesus, according to Paul.

To Paul's list of what cannot separate people from the love of God can be added ageing. Entering one's older years cannot separate a person from God's love in Christ Jesus. While the mere recitation of Paul's list may bring a person to a state of depression, especially as he or she reviews how many of the items on the list he or she has endured to old age, the apostle assures his readers that they are conquerors through God, who demonstrated his love for them by justifying them by faith in Jesus, who died and was raised by God.

While enduring privation, strain, harassment, hunger, the elements, injury, random acts of violence, or ageing cannot cut off people from God's love, they can send them into depression. But sadness caused by any of life's events or the other people in one's life are unable to separate one from God's love in Christ Jesus.

JOURNAL/MEDITATION: What has depressed you the most about getting older? What lifted you out of that depression?

PRAYER: Ever living God, your demonstrated your love in the resurrection of Jesus Christ, your Son. As a member of his body, I know that nothing can separate me from that love. When I am depressed because of my age, strengthen me with the confidence of Paul. I ask this through the same Christ Jesus, who is Lord forever and ever. Amen.

Old Age Afterbirth

SCRIPTURE: "The afterbirth of the body is old age, and you exist in corruption. You have absence as a gain. For you will not give up what is better if you depart. That which is worse has diminution, but there is grace for it. Nothing, then, redeems us from this world. But the All which we are, we are saved. We have received salvation from end to end. Let us think in this way! Let us comprehend in this way! (Treatise on Resurrection, p. 47, lines 18–31)

REFLECTION: "The Treatise on the Resurrection" is a document found in *The Nag Hammadi Library*, a collection of Gnostic scriptures, discovered in Egypt in 1945. "The Treatise on the Resurrection" was written near the end of the second century CE to deal with several questions for which Gnostic Christians sought answers. The document asserts that Jesus Christ destroyed death by his resurrection. Gnosticism taught that flesh was evil, and only thought or pure spirit was good. However, this document attests to the fact that the resurrected individual will, nevertheless, possess personally identifiable features. Also, the treatise teaches that people already participate in resurrection in the present.

The focus here is the image employed to describe old age. The treatise declares, "The afterbirth of the body is old age. . . ." While the metaphor may immediately send the elderly into a state of depression, there is a lot of truth to be mined in these words. From the moment of birth—even from the moment of conception—people begin to age. Just like there is afterbirth expelled by the mother after a person is born, the treatise declares that old age is a type of bodily afterbirth. This means that throughout one's life, one exists in corruption. This is a basic Gnostic teaching: All matter is evil.

From a Gnostic point of view, the absence of matter—body— is a gain. Giving up the body for pure thought is better. What is better is not remaining in the body; what is better is departing from the body. The body decreases with age and is, ultimately, done away with in death. Only grace, God's life, can resurrect a person—as pure spirit or thought—separate from his or her body. Thus, nothing redeems the body, which ages and dies.

The spirit or personality or whatever identifies one personally is saved by the All, God, who is pure thought. This is the salvation that has been given to people, according to the author of the treatise. Therefore, his readers should think these thoughts and understand resurrection as pure thought. Thus, while ageing is the afterbirth of the body and leads to death, it prepares a person for a new life of pure spirit or thought, which can be experienced now.

JOURNAL/MEDITATION: What is depressing to you about the quotation, "The afterbirth of the body is old age . . ."?

PRAYER: Lord Jesus Christ, when you were raised from the dead by your Father, you destroyed death. As I grow older in years and approach death, give me deeper faith in your resurrection. Ask the All, God, to save me with his grace. You live and reign with him and the Holy Spirit, one God, forever and ever. Amen.

Grieved in Spirit

SCRIPTURE: ". . . [A]t Ecbatana in Media, it . . . happened that Sarah, the daughter of Raguel, was reproached by one of her father's maids. For she had been married to seven husbands, and the wicked demon Asmodeus had killed each of them before they had been with her as is customary for wives. . . . [Sarah] was grieved in spirit and wept. When she had gone up to her father's upper room, she intended to hang herself. But she thought it over and said 'Never shall they reproach my father, saying to him, "You had only one beloved daughter but she hanged herself because of her distress." And I shall bring my father in his old age down to sorrow into Hades. It is better for me not to hang myself, but to pray the Lord that I may die and not listen to these reproaches anymore"' (Tob 3:7–8a, 10).

REFLECTION: The Book of Tobit is considered an Apocryphal or Deuterocanonical book by Jews and Protestants, but it is accepted as a canonical book in the Old Testament by Catholics and a few other denominations of Christians. It is a novel, written in the third century BCE, narrating the intertwined stories of Tobit, after whom the book is named, and Sarah, his future daughter-in-law, the future wife of his son, Tobias.

In the passage above, Sarah, daughter of Raguel—meaning "friend of God"—has been married seven times, but each husband dies on his wedding night before he can consummate the marriage. The narrator of the novel attributes the death of each husband to the demon named Asmodeus, an evil spirit of lust or carnal desire, whose name means "demon of wrath."

Sarah is reproached by one of her father's servants, who accuses her of killing her husbands on their wedding night. The young woman, who has become depressed, decides to hang herself in order to escape the accusations. However, after reflecting upon her intended action, she changes her mind; her deed would cause so much sorrow for her father in his old age that he would end up in Hades, the Greek name for the abode of the dead. The Jews referred to the abode of the dead as Sheol. In either case, it is important to note that this is not the Christian hell; it is merely the place where the dead live!

Sarah decides that it would be better for her to pray to the Lord that she might die and not have to suffer the reproaches of having lost seven husbands. She does pray, and God hears her prayer; he sends the (arch)angel Raphael, in the guise of one of her kinsmen, to arrange her marriage to Tobias and set her free from the wicked demon.

First, Sarah enters into depression, and rightly so after marrying seven men and not consummating her marriage with any one of them! Grieved in spirit, she thinks she has only one course of action left, namely, the self-destruction of her own life by hanging. But her father, Raguel, will have to bear the shame of her distress, so she changes her mind after thinking about what her intended deed will do to him.

Sarah's distress not only will affect her, but it will also affect her father in his old age. One person's depression affects other people, especially the elderly. So, while one may experience depression as a result of growing older, a younger's person's distress may dramatically affect the ageing. A spirituality of ageing awakens the one who is getting older to the consequences of depression. Such deep sadness not only affects the elderly, but it can affect others, too. Likewise, the elderly can be affected by the depression of the young. In the Book of Tobit, Sarah meets Tobias, marries him, and, after they pray together on their wedding night and burn a fish's liver and heart on the embers of incense—effectively driving away the demon—they consummate their marriage. The next morning, Tobias is discovered to be alive!

JOURNAL/MEDITATION: What depression in your old age has brought you close to suicide? What eliminated that option from your possibilities?

PRAYER: Blessed are you, O God of my ancestors, and blessed is your name in all generations forever. Let the heavens and the whole creation bless you forever. Remember me in times of distress, and look favorably upon me. Grant that I may experience your mercy and grow old in your grace. Amen.

Many Autumns

SCRIPTURE: "'Through many autumns have I toiled and labored, at night and morn, through age-inducing dawnings. Old age impairs the beauty of our bodies. Let husbands still come near unto their spouses" (Rig Veda 1:179.1).

REFLECTION: Hinduism's *The Rig Veda* contains a poem that is usually found in the appendix of the collection of hymns. The passage above represents the beginning of Hymn 179 from Book I. For the topic, the author chooses the depression associated with work or toil. He sings about working night and day. Each sunrise or dawn counts as another day of toil added to his age.

In order to further emphasize the fact of old age, the writer employs the metaphor of autumn, that time extending from the September equinox to the December solstice, when many living things decline or die in the Northern Hemisphere. As people progress through many autumns, the beauty of their bodies is impaired. Wrinkles appear on the forehead; skin is not as elastic as it once was; and once-limber fingers have trouble grasping a glass, mug, or spoon. Muscles are easily pulled, knees ache, and bones broken by a fall. Arteries become clogged, plumbing leaks, and control over other bodily functions is not as strong as it once was.

The hymn exhorts husbands to still approach their wives in old age. Verse 2, not quoted above, states, "[S]o now let wives come near unto their husbands." What the hymn suggests is that husband and wife should approach each other for sexual pleasure even in old age. In other words, when old age impairs the beauty of the body, the lack of beauty should not propel marriage partners away from each other.

Just to think about working day and night through many seasons into the autumn of one's life or one's retirement can be depressing. Add to that thought the fact that old age impairs the beauty of what was once a young body, and more depression can be added to what already exists. Such depression leads many people to all kinds of wrinkle-removing laser surgery, cosmetic surgery, hair implants for men, permanent hair removal for women, potency drugs, and on and on. A culture that prizes youth prompts the aged to remain looking young.

A spirituality of ageing, however, faces depression. It accepts the fact that the autumn of one's life has come. Some toil may be finished, but there is still some work to be done; in other words, there are still dawnings for days of labor. Furthermore, a spirituality of ageing acknowledges that old age impairs the beauty of the body. Such spirituality sees beauty in wrinkles, thinning hair, and impotence. A spiritual person is not depressed by old age; he or she understands it to be a different time for life.

JOURNAL/MEDITATION: What have you done to preserve the beauty of your body? In what ways have you come to see that many autumns of living leave a different kind of beauty etched in your flesh?

PRAYER: As I have toiled and labored, day and night, through many years and grown old, grant that I may enjoy the days of my retirement. Even though old age impairs the beauty of my body, may I come to a new appreciation of beauty that I share with others, especially my spouse. Amen.

chapter five

Acceptance

The maidens with long tresses hold him in embrace;
dead, they rise up again to meet the Living One.
Releasing them from age with a loud roar he comes,
filling them with new spirit, living, unsubdued.

—RIG VEDA 1:140.8

Delightful Old Age

SCRIPTURE: "Live your full lives and find old age delightful, all of you striving one behind the other. May Tvastar, maker of fair things, be gracious and lengthen out the days of your existence" (Rig Veda 10:18.6).

REFLECTION: Hymn 18 of book 10 in *The Rig Veda* contains the above verse about living a full life and finding old age delightful. The eldest, of course, usually reach the end of their journey before the youngest. The singer asks that Tvastar, Hinduism's first-born creator of the universe, be gracious and lengthen the days of one's life into old age.

Once a person has accepted the fact that he or she has attained sixty, seventy, eighty, or more years, he or she concludes that he or she has lived a full life. Old age is found to be delightful or pleasing, even as one is aware that he or she will follow others—family members and friends—to death. Since the creator made the person, the hymn-writer prays that the creator be gracious and lengthen the days of those who hear his song.

All one needs to do is look around to see others who find old age delightful. They are found as volunteers in many service organizations providing food to the hungry, clothing to the naked, and shelter to the homeless. They are found as ushers and ticket takers in theaters and performing arts centers where their presence indicates their love for the performing arts. Those who delight in old age teach children in religion classes, exercise with others in fitness centers, and assist the dying as hospice volunteers.

A full life overflows into other lives. Grandparents are often the source of vacations for their grandchildren, trips to amusement parks, and other types of adventures. Art museums often rely upon the experience of the elderly to lead tours and provide background for paintings and sculptures in their collections. Likewise, the curators of history museums know that living history in the persons of the elderly is more effective than examining old objects.

Those who find their old age delightful are clearly distinguished from those who have not accepted the total number of their years. These others complain about the weather, the traffic, and their adult children's child-rearing philosophy as it pertains to their grandchildren. They are too busy to volunteer in any capacity anywhere; they think that people should be paid for whatever work they do. Anything that might be fun is out of the question. Old age consists of years to be endured until death. Their lives do not bring life to others. A spirituality of ageing should lead the elderly person to share his or her life with others.

JOURNAL/MEDITATION: How has the acceptance of your age overflowed into others' lives?

PRAYER: May I embrace my older years graciously, as they lengthen the days of my existence. Grant that I may live a full life, finding old age delightful, overflowing with life into others' lives, even as I progress toward my death. Amen.

Generative Couple

SCRIPTURE: ". . . Abraham fell on his face and laughed, and said to himself, 'Can a child be born to a man who is a hundred years old? Can Sarah, who is ninety years old, bear a child?' God said, '. . . [Y[our wife Sarah shall bear you a son, and you shall name him Isaac. I will establish my covenant with him as an everlasting covenant for his offspring after him'" (Gen 17:17, 19).

REFLECTION: The Book of Genesis in the Hebrew Bible (Old Testament) contains a number of stories about the old generative couple named Abraham and Sarah. After Abraham hears God tell him that he and Sarah are going to give birth to Isaac, in separate stories both Abraham and Sarah laugh at so ridiculous an idea. Thinking to himself, in the above passage, the patriarch asks if a man one hundred years old can father a child, and if a woman ninety years old can conceive and bear a child. God says both are possible. Isaac will be born, and God will enter into covenant with him and his descendants.

Islam's *The Quran* also narrates this story several times. After hearing angels tell Abraham that he and Sarah will conceive and give birth to Isaac, Sarah says, "Woe betide me! Will I give birth when I am old and this my husband be aged? This is indeed surprising! (11:72) Later in the book, the author records visitors telling Abraham, "We bring you news of a son full of wisdom." Abraham answers them, "You bring me the good news now, when old age has come upon me. What good news are you giving me then?" "We have given you the happy tidings of a truth," they reply. "So do not be one of those who despair" (Quran 15:53b–55).

Abraham and Sarah bear witness to the truth that there is generativity in old age. While the intervention of God may be required for a hundred-year-old man and a ninety-year-old woman to conceive and bring to birth a child, there is a generativity of the elderly that should be included in a spirituality of ageing. Generativity describes the ability to create, generate, or produce something new.

Many people in their older years create their best painting, sculpture, and writing. Many learn how to play the piano, violin, or other musical instrument. Some older people are the best teachers; they are able to generate learning in their students. Because of their years of experience, the elderly, who have reflected upon and learned from experience, become the best counselors for others. Generativity can be seen on almost every TV evening news program, which narrates some outstanding feat accomplished by an older person.

The opposite of generativity is stagnation. Those who have arrived in their older years are finished with painting, sculpting, and writing. They are not interested in learning to play a musical instrument or in anything new. Because they have become set in their ways, they are the worst of teachers, using old notes and not adapting to new methods of teaching. Those who have reached stagnation know the answers to questions before they are asked by those younger than they. Stagnation is a type of living death.

Abraham and Sarah represent a concern for establishing the next generation. After Isaac is born, they continue their generativity by guiding him to keep the covenant God has established with him. This generative couple communicates a sense of optimism about humanity's future. Like Abraham and Sarah, those who have accepted their old age can be generative, too, in many ways.

JOURNAL/MEDITATION: In what specific ways do you demonstrate generativity in your older years?

PRAYER: God of Abraham and Sarah, from your chosen old couple you generated the life of Isaac. As I advance in my older years, bring about generativity in me that I may bear witness to your Holy Spirit at work in my life throughout all my days. Blessed are you, O God, for bringing new life out of old age, forever and ever. Amen.

Jacob's Twelve Sons

SCRIPTURE: "Now the sons of Jacob were twelve. The sons of Leah: Reuben (Jacob's firstborn), Simeon, Levi, Judah, Issachar, and Zebulum. The sons of Rachel: Joseph and Benjamin. The sons of Bilhah, Rachel's maid: Dan and Naphtali. The sons of Zilpah, Leah's maid: Gad and Asher. These were the sons of Jacob who were born to him . . ." (Gen 35:22b–26).

REFLECTION: In the Hebrew Bible's (Old Testament's) ancient patriarchal history, Abraham has two sons: Ishmael (whose mother was Hagar, Sarah's maid) and Isaac (whose mother was Sarah). Isaac becomes the father of Esau and Jacob, who stole the birthright from his older brother. Jacob marries two wives (Leah and Rachel) and considers each's maid (Bilhah, Zilpah) his concubine. To these four women twelve sons are born and one daughter named Dinah (cf. Gen 30:21). From the twelve sons arises the fiction of the twelve tribes of Israel, Jacob's other name (cf. Gen 35:10). The twelve tribes of Israel are a fiction because there is never a tribe of Joseph, whose descendants are divided into the half tribes of Ephraim and Manasseh.

Jacob's twelve sons represent a type of generativity. In ancient Hebrew and Israelite biology, the male was understood to carry the child in his sperm, what the ancients called seed—an agricultural metaphor. He planted the child in his wife or concubine, both of whom were considered to be fertile soil or incubators; if the female could not conceive, she was declared to be barren. The child grew in the womb for nine or ten months (they weren't exactly sure of the gestation period), until its life could be sustained outside the womb, and then it was born. Jacob generates sons (and a daughter). But, moreover, he generates the people of Israel, who will survive slavery in Egypt, a trek through the desert under the leadership of Moses, and take possession of the land promised by God to Abraham under the leadership of Joshua. In other words, Jacob generates a nation.

While many people in their older years will not generate a nation, they will often live to see their clan of grandchildren and great grandchildren and even great, great grandchildren. What Jacob illustrates is that from one person many are generated. Obituaries often attest to this fact: Jacob Jones, who married Leah Smith, died at the age of 94, having survived by four children, ten grandchildren, and three great grandchildren. Or Rachel Jones, who had been married to Jacob Smith for fifty-six years, died at the age of ninety-six, having survived by five children, twelve grandchildren, four great grandchildren, and one great, great grandchild.

A spirituality of ageing considers descendants. Because of two people's fruitfulness, many descendants have been generated. One's family tree has always been important because it indicates individual origins and community connectivity. Naming or identifying one's descendants is as important today as it was when the author of Genesis recorded Jacob's descendants.

JOURNAL/MEDITATION: Who are your descendants? How does each illustrate your generativity in your older years?

PRAYER: God of Jacob, from your chosen patriarch you brought forth a nation, a people you chose for your own. Bless my descendants with an outpouring of your grace, and grant that when my years are spent, I may be gathered with my ancestors into your presence, where you live forever and ever. Amen.

Life Preserver

SCRIPTURE: [Joseph said to the king's servant:] "'Sow as usual for seven years, and after reaping leave the corn in the ears, except the little you need for food. Then there will come seven years of hardship which will consume the grain you had laid up against them, except a little you may have stored away.' When the king heard this he said: 'Bring [Joseph] to me. I shall take him in my special service.' When he had talked to him, he said: 'Today you are established in a rank of trust with us.' 'Appoint me over the granaries of the land,' (he said); 'I shall be a knowledgeable keeper.' Thus We gave Joseph authority in the land so that he lived wherever he liked. We bestow Our favors on whomsoever We please, and do not allow the reward of those who are good to go [to] waste" (Quran 12:47–48, 54–56).

REFLECTION: Joseph, the eleventh of Jacob's twelve sons, is sold into Egyptian slavery by his brothers. However, because he has the ability to interpret dreams, he rises through the ranks of the Egyptian hierarchy to become second in command only to the reigning pharaoh. As the above text from *The Quran* explains, Joseph interprets the king's dream about seven years of plenty and seven years of famine, and the young Hebrew man is put in charge of storing grain during the years of plenty in order to have food during the years of famine.

    The Quran narrates Joseph's success in providing food for the Egyptians during the time of famine. Ultimately, Joseph's brothers and father migrate to Egypt to avoid the famine in their own land and share in the bounty Joseph has prepared in Egypt. *The Quran* declares that this demonstrates God's graciousness to whomever

he pleases. Joseph prays, "O my Lord, you have given me domin-
ion and taught me the interpretation of dreams; O Creator of the
heavens and the earth, You alone are my savior in this world and
the world to come; let me die submitting to You, and place me
among the upright" (Quran 12:101).

The author of the Book of Genesis in the Hebrew Bible (Old
Testament) interprets Joseph's action as God's way of saving the
world. Once Joseph, who is not at first recognized by his brothers
who have gone to Egypt to buy grain, reveals himself to them, he
calms their fear of any retaliation on Joseph's part for having sold
him into slavery by telling his brothers: ". . . Do not be distressed,
or angry with yourselves, because you sold me here; for God sent
me before you to preserve life. For the famine has been in the land
these two years; and there are five more years in which there will
be neither plowing nor harvest. God sent me before you to preserve for you a remnant on earth, and to keep alive for you many
survivors. So it was not you who sent me here, but God; he has
made me a father to Pharaoh, and lord of all his house and ruler
over all the land of Egypt" (Gen 45:5–8). Thus, the biblical Joseph
understands himself to be a life preserver.

A spirituality of ageing recognizes being a life preserver as a
type of generativity. Just like Joseph preserves the lives of Egyptians
and Hebrews alike, those in their older years often sustain the lives
of others. The elderly often welcome home their adult children
while they hunt for a job, providing both room and board. The
elderly often support the financial enterprises of others, helping
to make a down payment on a house, a car, or invest in a busi-
ness. Baby sitting services are often supplied by those in their older
years, as are visiting the sick, taking a meal to the homebound, or
driving a friend to a doctor's appointment. Like the Joseph in *The
Quran*, God is displaying his graciousness to others through the
elderly; like the Joseph in the Bible, God is preserving others' lives
through the elderly.

Journal/Meditation: In what specific ways are you an example
of God's graciousness? In what specific ways do you preserve lives?

PRAYER: Lord, God of Joseph, you bestow your graciousness upon whomever you please. Make me an instrument of your blessing to others. O Creator of the heavens and the earth, grant that I may always seek ways in my old age to preserve life. Help me to die submitted to you, who are God, forever and ever. Amen.

Old Age Birth

SCRIPTURE: "Then prayed Zachariah to his Lord: 'O Lord, bestow on me offspring, virtuous and good, for You answer all prayers.' Then the angels said to him as he stood in the chamber at prayer: 'God sends you good tidings of John who will confirm a thing from God and be noble, continent, and a prophet, and one of those who are upright and do good.' 'How can I have a son, O Lord,' he said, 'for I am old and my wife is barren?' 'Thus,' came the answer, 'God does as He wills'" (Quran 3:38–40).

REFLECTION: Both *The Quran* and the Bible narrate the birth of John the Baptist in the older years of Zachariah (Zechariah) and Elizabeth. In the above passage from *The Quran*, Zachariah prays to the Lord for a descendant, and angels bring good tidings that the old couple will give birth to John. Zachariah, however, asks how he, an old man, and Elizabeth, his old and barren wife, can conceive. The angels answer that God does as he wills.

In another account of the conception of John in *The Quran*, Zachariah, who describes himself as a very old man, calls to his Lord inwardly, saying, "'O my Lord, my bones decay, my head is white and hoary, yet in calling You, O Lord, I have never been deprived. But I fear my relatives after me; and my wife is barren. So grant me a successor as a favor from You who will be heir to me. . . .' 'O Zachariah,' (it was) said, 'We give you good news of a son by [the] name of John: To none have we attributed the name before.' 'How can I have a son, O Lord,' he said, 'when my wife is barren and I am old and decrepit?' (The angel) answered: 'Thus will it be. Your Lord said: "This is easy for Me; for when I brought you into being you were nothing."'" (Quran 19:4–9).

In both versions of the account found in *The Quran*, which was written in the early to middle seventh century CE, God brings life out of old age, because the Lord wills to do so, and because the Lord brings being out of nothing. In the Bible, specifically the Christian Bible's (New Testament's) Gospel According to Luke, written near the end of the first century CE, God brings life out of old age because nothing is impossible for God.

In Luke's Gospel, while Zechariah is serving as priest before God, the angel Gabriel appears to him and tells him that his prayer has been answered: Elderly Zechariah and his barren wife, Elizabeth, will conceive a son, who will be named John. Zechariah asks Gabriel, "How will I know that this is so? For I am an old man, and my wife is getting on in years" (Luke 1:18). John is conceived by old Zechariah and Elizabeth, and his conception is declared by Gabriel to be a demonstration that nothing is impossible with God (cf. Luke 1:36–37).

Luke's story is modeled on the account of the conception of Samuel in the Hebrew Bible (Old Testament). In this Deuteronomistic account, barren Hannah, Samuel's mother, prays to the LORD for a male child, promising to dedicate him to God as a Nazarite, that is, one who drinks no alcohol nor cuts his hair. The Dueteronomist records, "Elkanah knew his wife Hannah, and the LORD remembered her. In due time, Hannah conceived and bore a son. She named him Samuel . . ." (1 Sam 1:19b–20).

What do all these accounts have in common? People give birth in old age, because nothing is impossible for the LORD. While at times God may choose to violate the laws of basic biology, the truth remains even for those whose biological conception clock has stopped ticking in old age. Often, people hear about grandparents raising their grandchildren because of a divorce, imprisonment, or death of an adult child. Isn't that a type of giving birth in old age? Elders who coach soccer, football, baseball, ice skating, and other sports where the old are welcome, certainly give birth to athletes in old age. Another type of giving birth is helping parents take care of a sick child either at home or in the hospital. In these and in similar situations, who can say that God does not will these occurrences? A spirituality of ageing understands that people do give birth in old age.

JOURNAL/MEDITATION: To what or whom have you given birth in your old age?

PRAYER: O God, who do as you will, who bring into being out of naught, nothing is impossible for you. Bring to birth newness from my old age. Like Zechariah and Elizabeth, like Elkanah and Hannah, use me for your glory. Blessed are you, O LORD, forever and ever. Amen.

Virginal Old Age

SCRIPTURE: "Straightway, [while I (John) was contemplating these things,] behold, the [heavens opened and] the whole creation [which is] below heaven shone, and [the world] was shaken. [I was afraid, and behold I] saw in the light [a youth who stood] by me. While I looked [at him, he became] like an old man. And he [changed his] likeness (again) becoming like a servant. There was [not a plurality] before me, but there was a [likeness] with multiple forms in the light, and the [likenesses] appeared through each other, [and] the [likenesses] have three forms. He said to me, 'John, John, . . . I am the one who is [with you (pl.)] always. I [am the Father], I am the Mother, I am the Son. I am the undefiled and incorruptible one'" (Apocryphon of John, pg. 1, line 31–pg. 2, lines 9, 13–16; brackets and parentheses in the translation).

REFLECTION: "The Apocryphon of John," found in *The Nag Hammadi Library*, is a mythological Gnostic work from the second century CE. John, son of Zebedee, is the recipient of a revelation from the resurrected Christ. The work explains creation, fall, and salvation in Gnostic terms. In John's experience, as narrated above, the divine incorporates all ages and sexes into itself to reveal what complete humanity is supposed to be. The divine reveals itself not as three, but as one who is like a youth, an old man, and a servant.

John makes it clear that there is not a plurality, but merely multiple forms of likenesses. In other words, the divine incorporates in itself all ages.

Furthermore, the divine reveals that it contains both sexes and offspring. John hears the divine declare that it is the Father, the Mother, and the Son. That it is divine is expressed when John hears it say that it is undefiled and incorruptible. God is one, and that one contains male, female, and child. Thus, old age for both male and female is a manifestation of the divine.

In another Gnostic work from the second century CE, "The Testimony of Truth," also found in *The Nag Hammadi Library*, the author states the same point this way: "This, therefore, is the true testimony: When man comes to know himself and God who is over the truth, he will be saved, and he will crown himself with the crown unfading" (pg. 44, line 30–pg. 45, lines 1–7). The author then contrasts the conception of John the Baptist, one of the most important characters in Christianity—but an imperfect man— with the conception of Jesus. He writes: "John was begotten by the World through a woman, Elizabeth; and Christ was begotten by the world through a virgin, Mary. What is (the meaning of) this mystery? John was begotten by means of a womb worn with age, but Christ passed through a virgin's womb. When she had conceived, she gave birth to the Savior. Furthermore, she was found to be a virgin again" (pg. 45, lines 7–19).

John the Baptist was conceived through the sexual union of Zechariah and Elizabeth, his parents, in his mother's old womb. Christ—the perfect human—representative of the person who knows himself and God, was conceived in a womb that was virginal and remained so even after his birth. Christ's conception in the womb of the virgin demonstrates perfect humanity and perfect divinity united as one. According to Gnostic beliefs, people should lead a virginal life, foregoing marriage and sexual expression, in order to attain perfect humanity, knowing self and God as one.

This emphasis on leading a virginal life is displayed in the person of Joseph in "The Infancy Gospel of James," written in the second century CE. In this work, Mary is portrayed as a virgin *extra ordinaire.* In other words, she is portrayed as the perfect woman. To emphasize this, Joseph is portrayed as an old man, who takes Mary under his care and protection, but is absent when she conceives Jesus. At the age of three, Mary is brought to the temple by her parents, Joachim and Anna, where she lives until she is twelve years old, receiving her undefiled food from the hand of a heavenly messenger.

The high priest is told in a vision to gather the widowers, each of whom is to bring a staff. After gathering the staffs of the widowers, he enters the temple to pray. When he comes out, he hands the staffs back to their owners. When he hands Joseph's staff back to him, "Suddenly a dove [comes] out of this staff and perche[s] on Joseph's head. 'Joseph, Joseph,' the high priest said, 'you've been chosen by lot to take the virgin of the Lord into your care and protection.' But Joseph objected: 'I already have sons and I'm an old man; she's only a young woman. I'm afraid that I'll become the butt of jokes among the people of Israel.' And the high priest responded, 'Joseph, fear the Lord your God. . . .' And so out of fear Joseph took her into his care and protection. He said to her, 'Mary, I've gotten you from the temple of the Lord, but now I'm leaving you at home. I'm going away to build houses, but I'll come back to you. The Lord will protect you'" (Inf Gos Jas 9:6–9, 11–12).

Not only is Mary's perfect womanhood preserved by portraying Joseph as an old man, who leaves her at home to go build houses, but later in the story, after Mary gives birth to Jesus without any of the usual pain of birthing a child, Joseph declares to a midwife that she is his betrothed. He states, "I obtained her by lot as my wife. But she's not really my wife; she's pregnant by the Holy Spirit" (Inf Gos Jas 19:8). Furthermore, after the midwife examines Mary, she declares that "a virgin has given birth" (Inf Gos Jas 19:18).

These Gnostic texts attempt to present a spirituality of ageing that focuses on the perfect man, Christ, and the perfect woman, Mary. The metaphor used is virgin; it illustrates the patriarchal culture of the time which considered a woman a man's property. If she was not virginal, then she had been used. Virginity described a woman who had no experience of expressing herself sexually.

However, the metaphor upends the patriarchal culture by emphasizing the perfection of man and woman without sexual intercourse. The goal of marriage in the patriarchal culture was the production of children. The goal of virginity is the production of perfection. Here, the virginal one gives birth to life.

The model of perfection is found in John's vision of one who possesses no age, yet possesses all ages; the one who possesses no gender, yet possesses all genders; the one who possesses no children, yet possesses all children. From God's point of view, childhood, youth, middle age, and old age are one. From God's point of view, a human virgin gives birth to a divine, perfect creature. While one continues to bear the physical traits of male or female, a person transcends being male or female in a spirituality of ageing; one becomes a virgin, giving birth to life. This does not imply that the person is genderless, but it does mean that fathers become mothers, and mothers become fathers.

Journal/Meditation: In what ways have you transcended being male or female to become virginal? If you are male, how have you become female? If you are female, how have you become male?

Prayer: God who is One and Three, all time exists in you and both sexes are present in you. Through your divine Spirit, draw me beyond my gender to virginal old age. Grant that I may transcend maleness and femaleness to a perfect spirituality that reaches into eternity. I make this prayer in the name of the one who is perfect God and man, your Son, Jesus Christ, who is Lord, forever and ever. Amen.

Productive Old Age

Scripture: "The righteous flourish like the palm tree, and grow like a cedar in Lebanon. They are planted in the house of the LORD; they flourish in the courts of our God. In old age they still produce fruit; they are always green and full of sap, showing that the LORD is upright; he is my rock, and there is no unrighteousness in him" (Ps 92:12–15).

REFLECTION: The righteous man or woman is one who lives his or her life in a healthy relationship with the LORD. Biblical righteousness is one of the chief attributes of God. For people, it involves the right conduct or behavior; the words "ethical lifestyle" best capture the meaning of Hebrew Bible (Old Testament) righteousness.

Psalm 92 employs the metaphor of a tree to draw a picture of a righteous person. First, he or she is like a palm tree; the person thrives, grows hardy, and gives food and shelter. Second, the person is like a Lebanon cedar; he or she grows very tall. Third, the righteous man or woman flourishes permanently; he or she is like the long roots of a tree which reach deep into the soil. Each is firmly rooted in God's presence. When one reaches old age, he or she still produces the fruit of a righteous life; the person is green and full of sap, that is, alive in good deeds. Fourth, the fruitful production of righteousness in one's older years witnesses to God's righteousness or stability.

The lyrics of Psalm 92 echo the words of Moses to the Israelites in the Book of Deuteronomy in the Hebrew Bible (Old Testament). Moses tells the Israelites, who are preparing to invade the promised land, "You must follow exactly the path that the LORD your God has commanded you, so that you may live, and that it may go well with you, and that you may live long in the land that you are to possess" (Deut 5:33). Here, obedience to God's commands by walking in his ways will insure righteousness and long life on the promised land.

The Book of Wisdom in the Old Testament refers to this as understanding and a blameless life by the righteous. The author states, ". . . [O]ld age is not honored for length of times, or measured by number of years; but understanding is gray hair for anyone, and a blameless life is ripe old age" (Wis 4:8–9). Old age is not a measure of years, but it is measured by comprehending the deeper truths of life and by living according to them. "The righteous who have died will condemn the ungodly who are living, and youth that is quickly perfected will condemn the prolonged old age of the unrighteous" (Wis 4:16), declares the sapiential author.

A spirituality of ageing includes productivity in old age. While the fruit of old age can take many forms, it has several general characteristics. The way a person behaves indicates if he or she is following God's commandments, that is, walks in God's ways or on God's path. The person is stable, planted firmly as a tree. And he or she is wise, comprehending the deeper truths of life and living according to them. Such characteristics indicate a righteous individual, who is producing in old age.

Journal/Meditation: What are you producing in your older years that indicates you are living an ethical lifestyle?

Prayer: All that is within me blesses your holy name, O LORD. You crown me with steadfast love and mercy; you satisfy me with good as long as I live; you renew my youth like the eagle's. Keep me rooted firmly in your presence; keep me walking the way of your commands; fill me with your wisdom. Blessed may you be, O LORD, both now and forever. Amen.

Better with Age

Scripture: "Eleazar, one of the scribes in high position, a man now advanced in age and of noble presence, was being forced to open his mouth to eat swine's flesh. But he, welcoming death with honor rather than life with pollution, went up to the rack of his own accord, spitting out the flesh, as all ought to go who have the courage to refuse things that it is not right to taste, even for the natural love of life."

"Those who were in charge of that unlawful sacrifice took the man aside because of their long acquaintance with him, and privately urged him to bring meat of his own providing, proper for him to use, and to pretend that he was eating the flesh of the sacrificial meal that had been commanded by the king, so that by doing this he might be saved from death, and be treated kindly on account of his old friendship with them. But making a high resolve, worthy of his years and the dignity of his old age and the gray hairs that he had reached with distinction and his excellent life even from childhood, and moreover according to the holy God-given law, he declared himself quickly, telling them to send him to Hades."

"'Such pretense is not worthy of our time of life,' he said, 'for many of the young might supposed that Eleazar in his ninetieth year had gone over to an alien religion, and through my pretense, for the sake of living a brief moment longer, they would be led astray because of me, while I defile and disgrace my old age. Even if for the present I would avoid the punishment of mortals, yet whether I live or die I will not escape the hands of the Almighty. Therefore, by bravely giving up my life now, I will show myself worthy of my old age and leave to the young a noble example of how to die a good death willingly and nobly for the revered and holy laws.' When he had said this, he went at once to the rack" (2 Macc 6:18–28).

REFLECTION: The Old Testament's (Apocrypha's) Second Book of Maccabees, written by Jason of Cyrene, narrates some of the events of the martyrdom of Jews when Antiochus IV Epiphanes ruled Palestine in the second century BCE. In the short story above, Eleazar, a well-educated man who served as a scribe, that is, one who could write, is forced to eat pork in violation of Torah. Those commissioned with seeing that Jews, especially educated ones, shared in the sacrifice to a statue of Zeus that Antiochus had erected in the Jerusalem Temple, attempt to get Eleazar to pretend to eat the pork by substituting it with meat he was not forbidden to eat in order to save his life.

However, Eleazar refuses such a pretense because of honor and the example he would set for the young. Being ninety years old, Eleazar is a very disciplined man. He is venerated for his knowledge, guidance, wisdom, compassion, and existence. Eleazar is respected among his fellow Jews. Furthermore, he declares that he would give a bad example to the young; they would think that it was OK to violate the Torah in order to be self-centered and save their lives. Eleazar sees and lives by the bigger picture; he is mature, satisfied, and full of Torah and the divine spirit within it. Thus, he is able to renounce his life, because it makes no difference if he lives or dies; it is God's world, and even if he should escape death, he can never escape the LORD. Thus, Eleazar demonstrates that he is worthy of his ninety years and leaves an example to the young of how to die a good death, willingly and nobly, for a greater cause.

This biblical understanding of old age can be contrasted to the Western cultural understanding that old, gray-haired people are in the way. Older people possess a vision of life that the young have not yet experienced. Like Eleazar, they understand that there are some values in life that are worth one's life, that is, life is not the ultimate value that trumps all others. Age is not an obstacle to life; age is a gift to be shared with others. Eleazar shares honor with those who witness his death. It is better to die with honor than to live life without it. It is better to die than to give bad example to the young. Both honor and good example trump life. A spirituality of ageing must include those values that not only trump life, but also demonstrate how a person gets better with age.

Journal/Meditation: In what ways do you demonstrate that the values of honor and good example trump life?

Prayer: God of Eleazar, you gave your scribe the courage to witness to your Torah, even when it meant his own life. Give me that same valor that I might be a good example among the people I walk every day. Blessed be your name, O LORD, both now and forever. Amen.

Honor in Old Age

Scripture: "For one in the habit of showing respect, Of always honoring elder ones, Four qualities increase: Life, complexion, ease, and strength" (Dhammapada VIII:109).

REFLECTION: Buddhism's *The Dhammapada* contains important words about honor in old age. In the passage above, the person who shows respect and honor by greeting the aged receives an increase in life span. Along with the prolongation of life comes a better complexion, more ease, and more strength. In other words, anyone who honors an elderly person honors himself or herself, too.

Later, in Chapter XXIII, *The Dhammapada* states, "A blessing is virtue into old age, A blessing is faith established, A blessing is the attainment of insight-wisdom, A blessing it is to refrain from doing wrongs" (Dhammapdaa XXIII:333). The best adornment in old age is the practice of moral virtue, unshakable faith, attained insight that erupts into wisdom, and not doing deeds that are unwholesome. These practices honor old age.

In a lighter vein, *The Analects of Confucius* contain the following words about honor: "The Master said, Respect the young. How do you know that they will not one day be all that you are now? But if a man has reached forty or fifty and nothing has been heard of him, then I grant there is no need to respect him" (IX:22). In other words, honor is earned—no matter if one is young or old.

In the Bible, God tells Moses to tell the Israelites that one of his commandments is honor: "Honor your father and your mother, so that your days may be long in the land that the LORD your God is giving you" (Exod 20:12). In the Book of Leviticus, a collection of laws, God tells the Israelites: "You shall rise before the aged, and defer to the old; and you shall fear your God: I am the LORD" (19:32). And the Book of Proverbs preserves this saying: "Listen to your father who begot you, and do not despise your mother when she is old" (23:22). After the destruction of Jerusalem and the Israelites' deportation to Babylon, the prophet Zechariah tells the Jews: "Thus says the LORD of hosts: Old men and old women shall again sit in the streets of Jerusalem, each with staff in hand because of their great age" (8:4). What all of these biblical quotations have in common is the honor due the elderly, especially parents, in their old age.

The Quran speaks similarly: "So your Lord has decreed: Do not worship anyone but Him, and be good to your parents. If one or both of them grow old in your presence, do not say fie to them, nor reprove them, but say gentle words to them. And look after them with kindness and love, and say: 'O Lord, have mercy on them as they nourished me when I was small'" (17:23–24). The honoring of old parents is second only to prayer in the order of importance, according to *The Quran*. In Islam it is considered an honor to be able to care for one's old parents; it is an opportunity for great spiritual growth. According to *The Quran*, old Muslin parents are to be treated mercifully with kindness and selflessness by their children, never receiving a word of disrespect or scolding from them.

No matter how young or how old a person is, there will always be others who are older, and they deserve honor, which includes a good name, esteem, and respect. Such honor is earned through ethical conduct, keeping one's word, social interaction, and parenting. A spirituality of ageing includes honor of those who are older than oneself, no matter what one's age. When one honors another, he or she honors himself or herself.

JOURNAL/MEDITATION: In what ways do you honor those who are older than you? In what ways are you honored by those who are younger than you?

PRAYER: Lord, have mercy on the elderly, especially my parents. Grant me the awareness to recognize the older people around me and to honor their virtue, faith, and wisdom, that I may live a long life and be honored by those who come after me. You deserve all honor, O Lord, forever and ever. Amen.

Growing Old in God

SCRIPTURE: "Jesus said, 'The person old in days won't hesitate to ask a little child seven days old about the place of life, and that person will live'" (Gos Thom 4:1).

REFLECTION: "The Gospel of Thomas," a collection of 114 sayings of Jesus without a narrative structure, was created in the last third of the first century CE and went out of use by the end of the first century CE because narrative gospels (such as Mark, Matthew, Luke, John) had been written. The first verse of saying 4 above presents a paradox. The elderly are usually presented as wise, and children seven days old as unable to communicate. However, this saying turns the usual world upside down. In the verse above, the old person seeks the wisdom of life from the one who is not yet able to speak! Furthermore, the old seeker is promised life. The customary values of the world are reversed, because spirituality is not about always adhering to the world's values. In his or her innocence and inability to communicate, a child is able to teach an old person, who doesn't hesitate to ask, about the secrets of growing old in God to eternal life.

The psalmist prays similarly, taking refuge in the LORD, and imploring, "Do not cast me off in the time of old age; do not forsake me when my strength is spent" (Ps 71:9). Continuing his prayer for help, the singer begs, "So even to old age and gray hairs, O God, do not forsake me, until I proclaim your might to all the generations to come" (Ps 71:18). The LORD answers the psalmist's prayer in the prophet Isaiah. To the Jews in Babylonian captivity, who think that God has abandoned them, Isaiah portrays God telling the captives: "Listen to me, O house of Jacob, all the remnant of the house of Israel, who have been borne by me from your birth, carried from the womb; even to your old age I am he, even when you turn gray I will carry you. I have made, and I will bear; I will carry and [I] will save" (Isa 46:3-4). God does not forsake the elderly who grow old in him.

The wisdom of growing old in the God who carries one from birth, is also found in "The Thunder: Perfect Mind," a document of *The Nag Hammadi Library*. The title of the work indicates that it is wisdom that comes from God, the source of thunder, that leads to a perfect mind. In one among several "I am" verses, wisdom states, "I am the staff of his power in his youth, [and] he is the rod of my old age" (Thunder, pg. 14, lines 6-9). A rod is an elderly person's staff or cane. Thus, for the wise, God is the one upon whom the elderly lean and to whom they look for support.

Hinduism's *The Rig Veda* echoes this sentiment. In a long hymn dedicated to Indra, the supreme deity and god of heaven, rain, and thunder, the Hindu poet calls him the "Lord of Strength" upon whom he rests "as old men rest upon a staff" (8:45.20). In another hymn dedicated to Indra's brother, Agni, the poet seeks protection, declaring, "Old age, like gathering cloud, impairs the body: before that evil become nigh protect me" (Rig Veda 1:71.10). And in another hymn dedicated to Agni, the writer seeks protection on all sides, stating: "From rear, from front, from under, from above us, O King, protect us as a Sage with wisdom. Guard to old age thy friend, O Friend, Eternal: O Agni, as Immortal, guard us mortals" (Rig Veda 10:87.21).

From all these perspectives, it makes no difference if one worships God, the LORD, god, or gods. Those who grow old in their deity find the immortal one to be like a staff upon whom the elderly can lean and to whom they look for support. For those who understand this spirituality of ageing, this is wisdom, like that acquired from a seven-day-old child. Such wisdom leads to eternal life.

Journal/Meditation: How is your God or god like a staff or cane upon whom you lean for support?

Prayer: O God of heaven and earth, from whom all wisdom comes, let me never be separated from you. Grant that I may grow into old age with you as my staff for support. Then, I will proclaim your might to all the generations to come. You are God, forever and ever. Amen.

Gray Hair

Scripture: "The glory of youths is their strength, but the beauty of the aged is their gray hair" (Prov 20:29).

REFLECTION: The underlying presupposition of the above maxim from the Hebrew Bible (Old Testament) Book of Proverbs is that what is within is manifest without. Thus, youths reveal their inner strength in every type of sport, in work, and in learning. The aged reveal their inner glory and wisdom through their gray hair. Earlier, the collector of proverbs states, "Gray hair is a crown of glory; it is gained in a righteous life" (Proverbs 16:31). A righteous life, of course, is one lived in a healthy relationship with God.

The Dhammapada cautions Buddhism's adherents that gray hair does not always indicate maturity in wisdom. It states, "One does not become an Elder Because one's head is gray-haired; Ripened his age, 'Grown old in vain' is he called" (Dhammapada XIX:260). The qualities that make one an elder are found within a person; they are named in the next verse: "In whom there is truth and *dhamma*, Harmlessness, restraint, control, Who has the stains ejected, and is wise, He indeed is called 'Elder'" (Dhammapada XIX:261). Maturity in wisdom is displayed by the truth and virtue according to which one lives. More specifically, one is nonviolent, exercises self-restraint over the senses, and demonstrates self-control over himself or herself. The elder is one who has chosen a path of life and is steadfast in following it.

The wisdom of the Old Testament's (Apocrypha's) Book of Sirach also echoes that found in *The Dhammapada*. In the wisdom of Jesus, son of Sirach, otherwise known as the Book of Ecclesiasticus, the author exhorts his reader: "My child, from your youth choose discipline, and when you have gray hair you will still find wisdom" (6:18). In other words, one should choose discipline—a broad education with endured chastisement—in order to possess wisdom in old age. Wisdom requires commitment and fidelity when one is young, but the result is wisdom when one is old and gray.

A story in the Second Book of Maccabees in the Old Testament (Apocrypha) also illustrates gray-haired wisdom. Judas Maccabeus relates "a dream, a sort of vision, which was worthy of belief" (15:11), to his troops to prepare them for battle against Nicanor, a Syrian general under Antiochus IV Epiphanes and

Demetrius Soter, responsible for arresting Judas for his attacks on the Greek rulers of Palestine. In his vision, Judas sees the murdered Jewish high priest Onias III "praying with outstretched hands for the whole body of the Jews" (2 Macc 15:12). Judas continues narrating the vision: "Then in the same fashion another appeared, distinguished by his gray hair and dignity, and of marvelous majesty and authority. And Onias spoke, saying, 'This is a man who loves the family of Israel and prays much for the people and the holy city. . . .' Jeremiah [, the prophet of God,] stretched out his right hand and gave to Judas a gold sword, and as he gave it he addressed him thus: 'Take this holy sword, a gift from God, with which you will strike down your adversaries'" (2 Macc 15:13–16). After having stirred his troops with his vision, had this battle sanctioned by Jeremiah, and been distinguished by his gray hair and dignity, Judas, of marvelous majesty and authority, with God's gold sword, led his forces to victory over Nacanor on the Sabbath.

While Hymn 2 in Book 5 of *The Rig Veda* is dedicated to and describes the god Agni, one verse in particular applies to the theme of gray hair. The hymn writer states: "I saw him moving from the place he dwells in, even as with a herd, brilliantly shining. These seized him not: he had been born already. They who were gray with age again grow youthful" (Rig Veda 5:2.4). On the surface, the verse of the hymn compares the god of lightning and fire to the sun rising with a host of rays. Neither dawn nor dusk could stop him: Dawn could not stop him because the sun had already risen; dusk could not stop him because within a few hours the sun would return.

Pondering the last half of this stanza and comparing it to the words of wisdom quoted above, the reader may notice that he or she has grown gray with age and been reborn repeatedly throughout life. While every rebirth brings grayer hair, so does it bring youth. In other words, as a person passes through the stage of ageing, he or she navigates denial, anger, bargaining, depression, and acceptance over and over again. Once the process is finished, new birth and beautiful, youthful growth in virtue, truth, dignity, authority, and discipline occur—signified by gray hair.

JOURNAL/MEDITATION: What beautiful, youthful growth does your gray hair represent?

PRAYER: Ancient One, whose gray head and fiery throne represent your eternal and perfect wisdom, grant me successful new birth and youthful growth in every stage of my life. Keep me faithful to your path, that I may be declared righteous in your sight. You are God, forever and ever. Amen.

Length of Years

SCRIPTURE: ". . . [T]he LORD said, 'My spirit shall not abide in mortals forever, for they are flesh; their days shall be one hundred twenty years'" (Gen 6:3).

REFLECTION: One has to wonder if the writer of the sixth chapter of Genesis in the Hebrew Bible (Old Testament) had read the previous chapter! In chapter five, Adam is declared to have lived to be 930 years old (cf. Gen 5:5), and his son, Seth, lived to be 920 years old (cf. Gen 5:8). Other extraordinary long lives include Enosh, 905 (cf. Gen 5:11); Kenan, 910 (cf. Gen 5:14); Mahalalel, 895 (cf. Gen 5:17); Jared, 962 (cf. Gen 5:20); Enoch, 365 (cf. Gen 5:23); Methuselah, 969 (cf. Gen 6:27); Lamech, 777 (cf. Gen 5:31); Noah, 950 (cf. Gen 9:29); and Terah, 205 (cf. Gen 11:32). In the passage above, it looks like God decides to put a shorter limit on human life.

However, there is more to the number 120 than is at first obvious. In the ancient world, a life span was calculated to be forty years. Thus, forty became a number synonymous with a long time. Today it would be equivalent to saying, "Grandmother lived to be ancient." No one will conclude that she lived to be more than eighty, ninety, or maybe a hundred years old. When the number forty, meaning a life span or a long time, is multiplied by the number three, which designates the spiritual order, heaven, divinity, or God, the sum is 120. Thus, the LORD (three) declares that people will live three life spans (forty) before him.

Another point to which the reader should pay attention is the general decrease in ages. In the first years after creation, people lived to be over 900 years old. Now, they will live to be no more than 120. Later in biblical tradition, getting to seventy or eighty will be usual, as reflected in Psalm 90:10: "The days of our life are seventy years, or perhaps eighty, if we are strong." In other words, as human sin multiplies on the earth, human life span decreases on the earth.

However, the ages of the patriarchs do not reflect the 120-year limit. Abraham lives to be 175 (cf. Gen 25:7), which means he lived at least four life spans plus fifteen years of the fifth one. His wife, Sarah, lives to be 127 (cf. Gen 23:1), fulfilling the three-life span rule with the addition of seven more years; seven (the adding together of the spiritual order [three] and the created order [four]) indicates completeness or perfection). Abraham's and Hagar's son, Ishmael, lives to be 137 (cf. Gen 25:17) and Abraham's and Sarah's son, Isaac, lives to be 180 (cf. Gen 35:28), that is, four and half life spans. Jacob makes it to 147 (cf. Gen 47:28), while, Joseph, his son, lives to be 110 (cf. Gen 50:22, 26), ten years shy of the LORD's decreed life span. The Book of Deuteronomy declares that Moses lived exactly 120 years (cf. 34:7), achieving perfection in God's service.

Most of the time the Bible, like all other sacred literature, states that people lived into old age, acquired length of years, or reached a ripe old age to indicate that they were very old at death. As the author of Sirach states, "O death, how welcome is your sentence to one who is needy and failing in strength, worn down by age and anxious about everything; to one who is contrary, and has lost all patience!" (41:2) No matter the length of one's years, every person's life ends in death. Knowing this fact and reflecting upon it is what enables people to embrace life and live.

Maybe it is at seventy, eighty, or ninety that a person recognizes that he or she is old. Certainly, physical strength decreases, mental acuity is somewhat slowed, emotional stability may totter, psychologically one comes to terms with his or her age, what used to give pleasure aesthetically no longer does so, sexual potency no longer exists, but the spiritual aspect needs nourishment so that the person becomes full of maturity and satisfied. In other words, one gets in the closest or in the deepest touch possible with the divine or eternal spirit within him or her. That life force or soul is what exists once one's years have come to an end.

A person's spirituality of ageing notices that all things and beings are interconnected. All life is sacred, and all life is one. Ageing is not a cause for retirement from life, but it becomes the opportunity to discover the meaning of life and self in depth. One is not alone in this process; others who are ageing are walking the same path. In this universal process of ageing, there is plenty of company with whom to share one's spirituality of ageing, enriching others' lives and having one's own enriched by them.

JOURNAL/MEDITATION: To what age do you hope to live? How do others' ripe old ages inspire you to continue on your path of a deeper spirituality of ageing?

PRAYER: God of all ages, the days of my life are seventy years, or perhaps eighty, if I am strong. Deepen my wisdom, that I may continue to walk according to your ways, reach maturity, and be satisfied with you grace. To you, who are beyond years, be honor, glory, and praise, forever and ever. Amen.

chapter six

Synthesis

It is God who creates you, then makes you die;
and some reach the age of dotage,
so that once having known
they do not know a thing.
God is indeed all-knowing and all-mighty.

—QURAN 16:70

1. Review your journal/meditation entries for chapter 1 on denial. If you want, you may share them either in written or oral form with another person, who may be able to help you answer the following questions: What theme do you find embedded in or underlying your journal/mediation entries? What did you deny about getting older? What supported your denial? What helped you accept the fact of your ageing and stop denying it? Record your answers to the synthesis of your journal/mediation entries for chapter 1 in your journal, because you will be using them later.

2. Review your journal/meditation entries for chapter 2 on anger. If you want, you may share them either in written or oral form with another person, who may be able to help you answer the following questions: What theme do you find embedded in or underlying your journal/mediation entries? How did you express anger at ageing? What helped you recognize or name your anger? Record your answers to the synthesis of your journal/mediation entries for chapter 2 in your journal, because you will be using them later.

3. Review your journal/meditation entries for chapter 3 on bargaining. If you want, you may share them either in written or oral form with another person, who may be able to help you answer the following questions: What theme do you find embedded in or underlying your journal/mediation entries? What were you willing to bargain? Record your answers to the synthesis of your journal/mediation entries for chapter 3 in your journal, because you will be using them later.

4. Review your journal/meditation entries for chapter 4 on depression. If you want, you may share them either in written or oral form with another person, who may be able to help you answer the following questions: What theme do you find embedded in or underlying your journal/mediation entries? What characterized your depression? What helped to lift you out of depression? Record your answers to the synthesis of your journal/mediation entries for chapter 4 in your journal, because you will be using them later.

5. Review your journal/meditation entries for chapter 5 on acceptance. If you want, you may share them either in written or oral form with another person, who may be able to help you answer the following questions: What theme do you find embedded in or underlying your journal/mediation entries? What do you find delightful about ageing? What do you find generative about ageing? What characterizes ageing for you? What new life have you found as a result of accepting the fact of your ageing? Record your answers to the synthesis of your journal/mediation entries for chapter 5 in your journal, because you will be using them later.

6. From your synthesis of each chapter of the book that you have recorded in answers to questions 1 through 5 above, in five simple steps carefully name and plot your denial of ageing, anger at ageing, bargaining with ageing, depression at ageing, and acceptance of ageing? What do observe about your steps? Record this information in your journal.

7. Spirituality, as a way of life, transforms, transfigures, the person step-by-step as he or she gets closer and closer to the divine—however one chooses to name it. After meeting the divine, the individual better understands all of the circumstances of his or her life, including his or her unique self. Spirituality is the way that one is in the divine's presence, which emerges through human experiences of ageing. In a sentence or two, answer this question in your journal: What is your spirituality of ageing? You'll find this in synthesized form in your answer to question 6 above.

8. The following are ten quotes for further reflection on ageing from a variety of sources other than the literature of world religions. Spend time with them to see if they further deepen your own spirituality of ageing or tweak it in some way.

a. "I feel thin, sort of stretched, like butter scraped over too much bread." (Bilbo to Gandalf in *The Lord of the Rings: The Fellowship of the Ring* by J. R. R. Tolkien)

b. "It's not how old you are; it's how you are old." (Jules Renard)

c. "Death is coming—but hopefully not before old age, decrepitude, and senility." (Jarod Kintz, *This Book Title Is Invisible*)

d. "The complete life, the perfect pattern, includes old age as well as youth and maturity. The beauty of the morning and the radiance of noon are good, but it would be a very silly person who drew the curtains and turned on the light in order to shut out the tranquility of the evening. Old age has its pleasures, which, though different, are not less than the pleasures of youth." (W. Somerset Maugham, *The Summing Up*)

e. "As we grow older, we must discipline ourselves to continue expanding, broadening, learning, keeping our minds active and open." (Clint Eastwood)

f. "It seems only the old are able to sit next to one another and not say anything and still feel content. The young, brash and impatient, must always break the silence. It is a waste, for silence is pure. Silence is holy. It draws people together because only those who are comfortable with each other can sit without speaking. This is the great paradox." (Nicholas Sparks, *The Notebook*)

g. "When you're five, you know your age down to the month. Even in your twenties you know how old you are. I'm twenty-three, you say, or maybe twenty-seven. But then in your thirties something strange starts to happen. It's a mere hiccup at first, an instant of hesitation. How old are you? Oh, I'm—you start confidently, but then you stop. You were going to say thirty-three, but you're not. You're thirty-five. And then you're bothered, because you wonder if this is the beginning of the end. It is, of course, but it's decades before you admit it." (Sara Gruen, *Water for Elephants*)

h. "The great renunciation of old age as it prepared for death, wraps itself up in its chrysalis, which may be observed at the end of lives that are at all prolonged, even in old lovers who have lived for one another, in old friends bound by the closest ties of mutual sympathy, who, after a certain year, cease to make the necessary journey or even to cross the street to see one another, cease to correspond, and know that they will communicate no more in this world." (Marcel Proust, *Swann's Way*)

i. "The art of growing old is the art of being regarded by the oncoming generations as a support and not as a stumbling-block." (Andre Maurois, *An Art of Living*)

j. "It is because the old have forgotten life that they preach wisdom." (Philip Moeller, *Helena's Husband*)

After reflection on any quotations that caught your attention, record your thoughts in your journal. Do your reflections spark you to revise your spirituality of ageing. If so, in your journal record your revised spirituality of ageing.

Bibliography

Miller, Robert J. "The Gospel of Thomas." In *The Complete Gospels: Annotated Scholars Version*. San Francisco: HarperSanFrancisco and Polebridge Press, 1992, 1994.

———, ed. "The Infancy Gospel of James." In *The Complete Gospels: Annotated Scholars Version*. San Francisco: HarperSanFrancisco and Polebridge Press, 1992, 1994.

O'Day, Gail R., and David Peterson, eds. *The Access Bible: New Revised Standard Version with the Apocryphal/Deuterocanonical Books*. New York: Oxford University Press, 1999.

Pelikan, Jaroslav, ed. *Sacred Writings, Volume 3, Islam: The Quran*. Translated by Ahmed Ali. New York: Book-of-the-Month Club, 1992.

———. *Sacred Writings, Volume 4, Confucianism: The Analects of Confucius*. Translated by Arthur Waley. New York: Book-of-the-Month Club, 1992.

———. *Sacred Writings, Volume 5, Hinduism: The Rig Veda*. Translated by Ralph T. H. Griffith. New York: Book-of-the-Month Club, 1992.

———. *Sacred Writings, Volume 6, Buddhism: The Dhammapada*. Translated by John Ross Carter, Mahinda Palihawadana. New York: Book-of-the-Month Club, 1992.

Reorganized Church of Jesus Christ of Latter Days Saints, The. *Book of Doctrine and Covenants*. Independence, MO: Board of Publication of the Reorganized Church of Jesus Christ of Latter Day Saints, 1947.

Robinson, James M., ed. "The Apocryphon of John." Translated by Frederik Wisse. In *The Nag Hammadi Library in English*. Third Revised Edition. San Francisco: HarperSanFrancisco, 1978, 1988, 1990.

———. "The Testimony of Truth." Translated by Soren Giversen, Birger A. Perason. In *The Nag Hammadi Library in English*. Third Revised Edition. San Francisco: HarperSanFrancisco, 1978, 1988, 1990.

———. "The Thunder: Perfect Mind." Translated by George W. MacRae. In *The Nag Hammadi Library in English*. Third Revised Edition. San Francisco: HarperSanFrancisco, 1978, 1988, 1990.

———. "The Treatise on the Resurrection." Translated by Malcolm L. Peel. In *The Nag Hammadi Library in English*. Third Revised Edition. San Francisco: HarperSanFrancisco, 1978, 1988, 1990.